LOVE & HATE
IN AMERICA TODAY

Books in the YOUTH WORLD Series

Popular Song & Youth Today

Contemporary Film & the *New* Generation

Peace, War & Youth

Getting High Naturally

Touch With Love

Love & Hate in America Today

LOVE & HATE
IN AMERICA TODAY

Edited by
Louis M. Savary

Association Press
New York, N.Y.

LOVE & HATE IN AMERICA TODAY
Copyright © 1971 by Association Press
291 Broadway, New York, N.Y. 10007

All rights reserved. No part of this publication may be reprinted, reproduced, transmitted, stored in a retrieval system, or otherwise utilized, in any form or by any means, electronic or mechanical, including photocopying or recording, now existing or hereinafter invented, without the prior written permission of the publisher.

Standard Book Number: 8096-1820-6
Library of Congress Catalog Card Number: 78-152899

Printed in the United States of America

ACKNOWLEDGMENTS

Many of the works from which selections herein are taken are protected by copyright, and may not be reproduced in any form without the consent of the authors, their publishers, or their agents. Every effort has been made to trace the ownership of all selections in this book and to obtain the necessary authorization for their use. If any errors or omissions have occurred in this regard, corrections will be made in all future editions of this book. Since the copyright page cannot legibly accommodate all the acknowledgments and copyright notices, this page and the pages following constitute an extension of the copyright page.

Grateful acknowledgment is made to: Addison-Wesley Publishing Co., Inc. for selection by Gordon W. Allport from *The Nature of Prejudice*, 1954; *America* for selection by Robert O. Johann; *The Atlantic* for selection by Robert J. Lifton from "The Young and The Old," 1969; Jonathan Black for selection from "The Radical Lawyer," 1970; *Caller-Times*, Corpus Christi, for selection by Edward H. Harte; Jonathan Cape, London, for selection by Claude Brown from *Manchild in the Promised Land*, 1966; *Careers Today* for selections by Morris B. Abram and Craig Vetter; *Childhood Education* for selection by Hilda Taba from "How Adults Influence Children"; Chilton Co., Publishers for selections by Erich Fromm reprinted in A. J. Marrow's *Changing Patterns of Prejudice*, 1962; *Christians Only* for selection by Heywood Broun; Clube de Poesia do Brasil for poem by João Accioli from *An*

Introduction to Modern Brazilian Poetry, 1954; *The Commonweal* for selection by Jacques Maritain; Cowles Syndicate for permission to reprint selection by Fletcher Knebel from "The Wasps: 1968." Fletcher Knebel, Look Magazine © 1968; Doubleday & Company, Inc. for selection by Margaret Mead from *Culture and Commitment: A Study of the Generation Gap*, 1970; Karen Durgin for selections from "Women's Liberation," 1970; Ira Einhorn for selection from "Change, Media, Communication," 1970; *Facts* for selection by George L. Rockwell, 1963; Grove Press, Inc. for selection by Frantz Fanon from *The Wretched of the Earth*, 1965, and for selection by Malcolm X from *Autobiography of Malcolm X*, 1966; Guerrilla Art Action Group for selection by John Hendricks from "Toward a New Humanism," 1970; Harcourt, Brace, Jovanovich, Inc. for selection by Konrad Lorenz from *On Aggression*, 1966, and for selection by George Orwell from *Animal Farm*, 1946; Harlem Youth Opportunities Unltd., Inc. for selection by Harlem girl, age 15; Harper & Row, Publishers for selections by Martin Buber from *Collected Essays*, 1957, and selection by Arthur C. Clarke from *Profiles of the Future*, 1958, and selection by Robert L. Heilbroner from *The Great Ascent*, 1963, and selection by John F. Kennedy from *Profiles in Courage*, 1964, and for selection by Pierre Teilhard de Chardin from *The Phenomenon of Man*, 1959; Ione Hill for permission to reprint poems from *Three-Eyed Pieces*, 1967, and *Strangers Eye-Kiss*, 1969; *Hit Parader* for selections by Neil Diamond and John Kay; Houghton Mifflin Co. for selection by Romain Rolland from *The Making of the Modern Mind* by John Herman Randall, Jr., 1940; Martin Jezer for selections from "Family, Tribe and the Quest for Community," 1970; Alfred A. Knopf, Inc. for selection by Albert Camus from *The Rebel*, 1956, and selections by Stokely Carmichael and Eldridge Cleaver from *Black Power*, ed. by S. S. Carmichael and C. V. Hamilton, 1967, and selections by Kahlil Gibran from *The Prophet*, 1923, and for selection by John O. Killens from *Black Man's Burden*, 1969; *Ladies' Home Journal* for selection by Benjamin Spock from "Do Parents Teach Prejudice?"; Little, Brown and Company for permission to reprint selection by Ogden Nash from his poem "Bankers are just like anybody else, except richer." Copyright © 1935 by Ogden Nash, which originally appeared in *The New Yorker; Look* for selection by Edward H. Flannery, and for selections from Sunday-school lessons reprinted in James A. Pike's "The Roots of Bias," 1961; *Marriage* for selection from Norman Thomas; Kathy Mulherin for selection from "Ties That Bind," 1970; The New American Library for selection by Thomas A. Dooley from *The Edge of Tomorrow*, 1958; New

Directions Publishing Corp. for selection by Gary Snyder from *Earth House Hold*, 1969; *The New Republic* for selection by Martin Duberman; *The New York Review of Books* for selection by I. F. Stone; *The New York Times* for selections by Anthony Carthew, Betty Friedan, Whitney Young, Daniel P. Moynihan; *Newsweek* for selection by Seabury H. Ford; Oceana Press, Inc. for selection by Gerald L. K. Smith reprinted in *The Hate Reader*, ed. by Edwin S. Newman, 1964; Alan Oken for selection from "The Age of Aquarius," 1970; Opara for his selection from "The Blacks," 1970; Oxford University Press for selection by Erich Frank from *Philosophical Understanding and Religious Truth*, 1945; Random House, Inc. for the selection by Jonathan Eisen from *The Age of Rock: Sounds of the American Cultural Revolution*, 1969, and for selection by Charles Silberman from *Crisis in Black and White*, 1964; *Redbook Magazine* for selections by Cheryl Henderson, Roberta Madden, and P. B. Frank; *Saturday Review* for selections by Max Birnbaum, Libby Benedict, Thedford Slaughter; *Survey Graphic* for selection by Oscar I. Janowsky; *Theology Digest* for selection by Paul J. Weber, S.J., 1969; *Think* for selection by Robert L. Heilbroner from "Don't Let Stereotypes Warp Your Judgment," 1961; *Time* for selections by Jewel Drake, Constance Hilliard, Thomas P. O'Neill, Jerry Weisgraw, Roy Wilkins; Viking Press, Inc. for selection by Ruth Benedict and Gene Weltfish from *The Races of Mankind*, 1945; World Publishing Co., for selection by David Ben-Gurion from his *Memoirs*, 1970.

Photo Credits: American Jewish Committee 15, 48-49, 52-53, 77, 78-79, 80, 83, 85, 86, 88, 90, 95; Karen Becker 18-19, 26, 158-159; Leslie Becker 189; Ettie deLáczay 120; Valentine Echo 34-35; Maury Englander 170-171; Laurence Fink 61, 69, 118, 160, 175, 185; P. J. J. Fortin 20-21, 44, 56, 64, 127; Cynthia Grey 22-23, 176-177, 182-183; Seymour Linden 33, 180; Fortune Monte 98; Sylvia Plachy 131, 141, 148, 187; Abe Rezny 39, 55; Shelly Rusten 12, 25, 28, 36, 40-41, 59, 74, 102, 104-105, 108-109, 124-125, 128-129, 151, 154, 156; David Sagarin 31, 63, 100, 107, 113, 116, 134, 144-145, 153, 169, 179, 191; Standard Oil (N.J.) 167; Swedish Travel Office 163; Swiss National Tourist Office 72, 93, 133; U.S. Rubber 16; Wayne Wiebel 47, 51, 67, 122, 138, 143, 146-147, 173.

CONTENTS

Preface 9

1. The Camera's Point of View
   Feeling Prejudice 13
   Values 23
   The Challenge to Civilization 29

2. Black and White
   The Situation for Blacks 45
   Doing Something About the Crisis 57
   The Destiny of Brothers 65

3. Let My People Go
   The Religious Condition 73
   The Case of Anti-Semitism 81
   Religious Response to Religious Prejudice 91

4. A Woman's Place
   Freud as Public Enemy 99
   The Least Finished Revolution 105

5. Rich Man, Poor Man
   Complaints From Various Quarters 112
   Home: Darkness and Light 121
   Beginning the Ascent 129

6. Generations Apart
    Parents and Other Strangers   139
    What We Are Doing   149
    Points of Convergence   157

7. A New History of Man
    Teaching and Learning   166
    Love With Power   174
    The All Together   183

PREFACE

At its roots, prejudice is a matter of hatred and ignorance where there should be love and understanding. America today is caught in a struggle between these two sets of forces. People experience prejudice in their daily lives in many forms: in conflicts between racial groups, in antipathy toward religious minorities, in feelings pro and con about women's liberation, in the struggle for power and property and status, in the gulf of misunderstanding between generations. In many ways, America today is a house divided.

Everywhere ignorance and hatred are factors in American life. And although people with understanding hearts try to ease tensions and to help open minds that are closed, they often do not know how to show others the way to replace hate with love. Social critics, who have learned how to isolate and break down negative and destructive attitudes, seldom know how to build positive perspectives. They know how to diminish prejudice, but they rarely do anything to create new value systems.

The problem of prejudice is therefore not merely the problem of dealing with fear, defiance and rejection. There must be a personal and common effort to achieve understanding, cooperation, trust. This work has hardly begun—but in the American melting pot there are large possibilities for experiment. And today there are new people at work, people with young spirits who want to create a new history of man.

1

THE CAMERA'S POINT OF VIEW

Feeling Prejudice

Interviewer: Why do we have a flag?
Child: God made it so they'd know who was the good people.

    The New York Times Magazine

Severely bruised and with blood streaming from His body, Jesus was presented to the Jews by Pilate with the pitying appeal, "Behold the Man." ... The hardhearted, unbelieving Jews could not even thus be moved to pity.

A Sunday-School Lesson

Most of the Negro people in this country
are in complete agreement with the Muslims
    and their ideals
just as most of the white people in this country
are in agreement with the Nazis.
The only job before us is
to remove their fear
and set them free to join us.

George Lincoln Rockwell

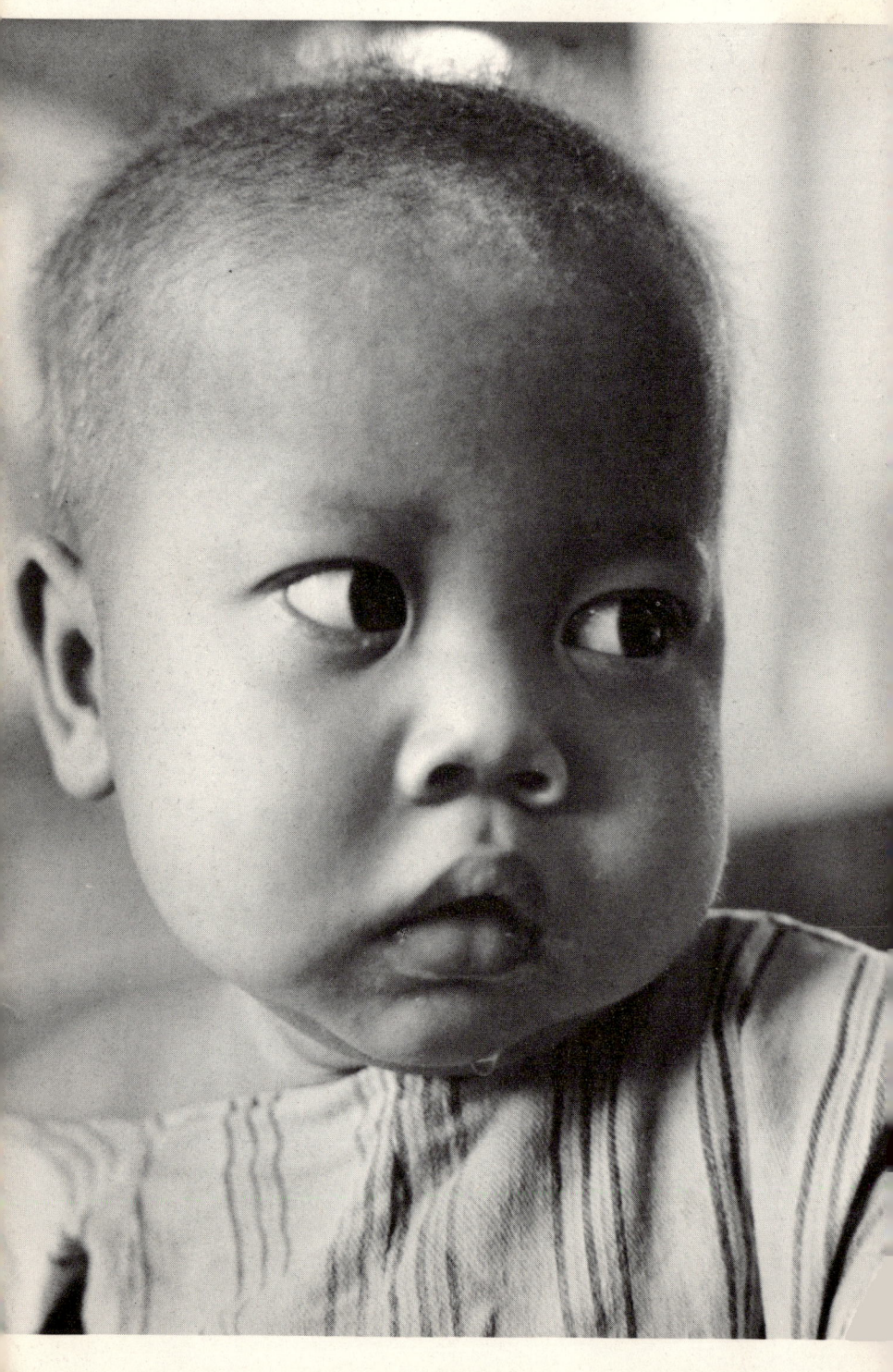

How would you like to have
the bloodstream of your baby,
or your son, or daughter, or wife
polluted by dried blood
collected from Jews, Negroes,
and criminals?

    Gerald L. K. Smith

It has been said that in Northern Ireland
Catholics are blacks who happen to have white
    skins.

                      Anthony Carthew

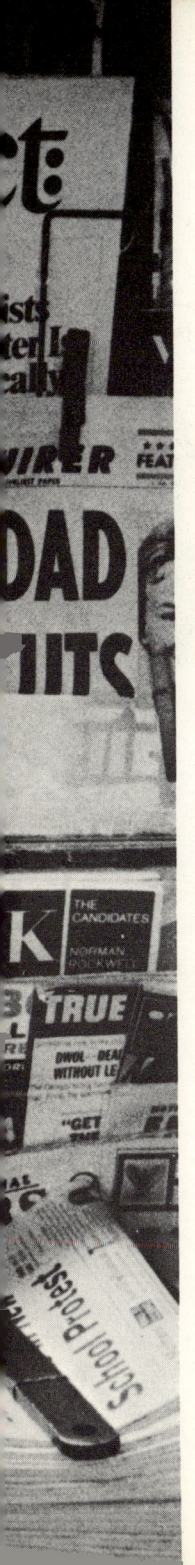

Then what is man? And what man seeing this,
And having human feelings, does not blush
And hang his head, to think himself a man?

William Cowper

What a contradiction man is!
    Judge of all things,
feeble worm of the earth,
    depository of truth,
a sink of uncertainty and error,
    the glory and shame of the universe.

Blaise Pascal

The hating person seems to have
a feeling of relief,
as though he were happy
to have found the opportunity
to express his lingering hostility . . .
the passion to destroy or cripple life.

                Erich Fromm

And as a single leaf
turns not yellow
but with the silent knowledge
of the whole tree,
So the wrong-doer
cannot do wrong
without the hidden will
of you all.

              Kahlil Gibran

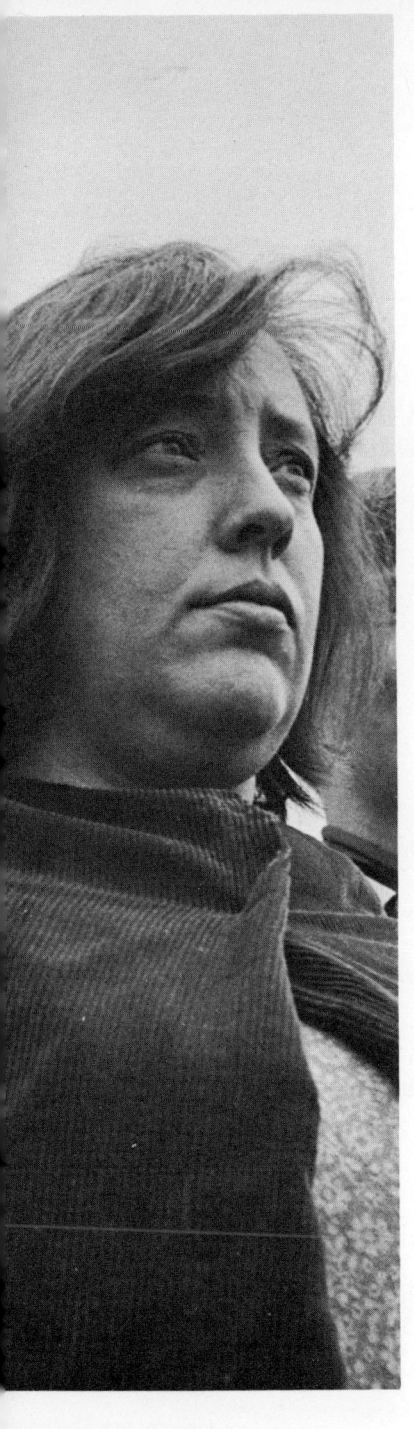

Values

The camera does not lie;
But even the camera
Is limited to
Its point of view.

        Ione Hill

Life revolves
around one's philosophy
and personality.
Through one you receive,
and through the other
you give.
One represents thinking
and the other action;
for as you think
so will you act.
Thus, what you think
about life,
and the way you respond to it
really matters.
Life is as simple as this.

        William H. McClurg

In a society in which there is general agreement
on what constitutes the good, the true, and the beautiful,
the task of teaching values is a simple one.
The consensus is clear
and, even if minority views exist,
they do not challenge
the majority judgment effectively.
But in a pluralist society,
in which no general agreement
has been reached, the problem
becomes infinitely more difficult.

Teaching values
in American classrooms today, therefore,
is an awesome assignment.
For, as a nation, we are caught
between the myths of a rural past
that has all but disappeared,
and the new urban present
that has not yet achieved its final form.
While our backs were turned,
profound changes took place
not only in our values,
but in the very sources from which they come.

      Max Birnbaum

Insecurity creates fear;
fear results in intolerance;
and intolerance is the mother of inhumanity.

                Oscar I. Janowsky

I the Lord search the mind
and try the heart,
to give to every man
according to his ways,
according to the fruit of
his doing.

                Jeremiah 17:10

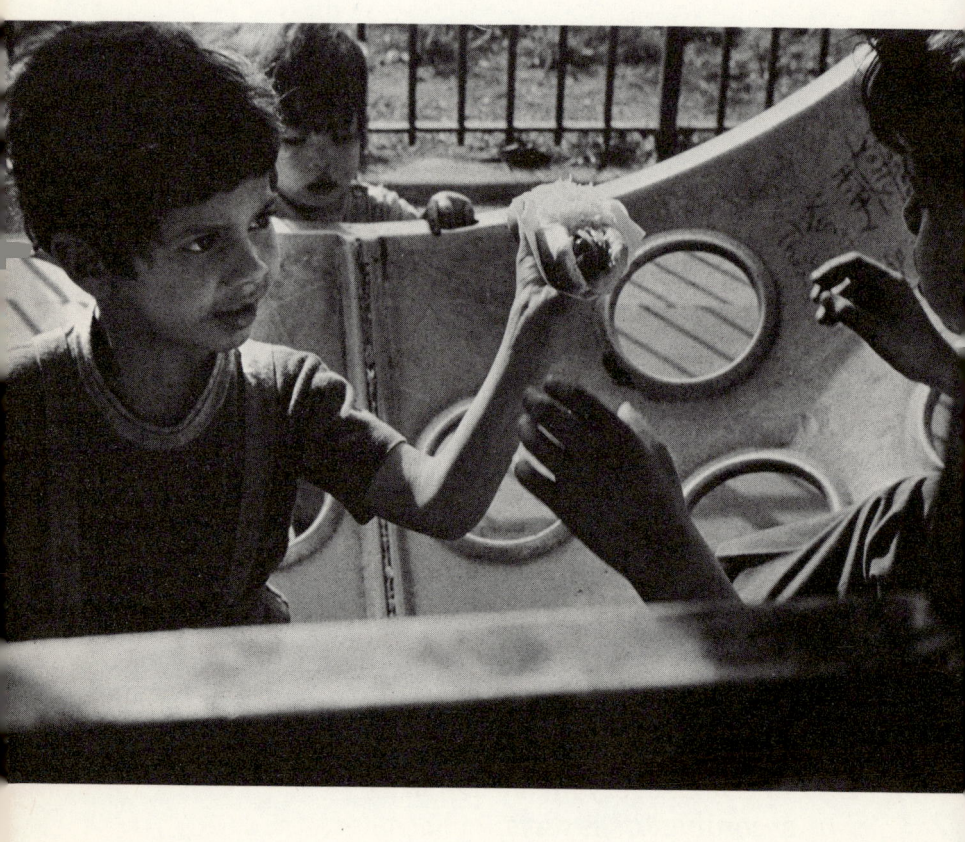

The Challenge to Civilization

We hold these truths to be self-evident;
that all men are created equal,
that they are endowed by their creator
with certain inalienable rights,
that among these are life, liberty
and the pursuit of happiness.
That to secure these rights,
governments are instituted among men,
deriving their just powers
from the consent of the governed.

> Declaration of Independence

In a healthy democracy
the majority and the nonconformist
depend upon each other,
and each supplies a vital component
to the whole.
Stability is provided by the majority,
while vitality flows from the nonconformist,
not merely as an act of decency,
but more significantly
as an imperative for himself
and the whole society.

> John P. Roche

"When I use a word," Humpty Dumpty said in a rather scornful tone, "it means just what I choose it to mean—neither more nor less."

"The question is," said Alice, "whether you *can* make words mean so many different things."

"The question is," said Humpty Dumpty, "which is to be master—that's all."

Lewis Carroll

That peoples can no longer
carry on authentic dialogue
with one another
is not only the most acute symptom
of the pathology of our time,
it is also that which most urgently
makes a demand of us.
I believe, despite all,
that the peoples . . .
can enter into dialogue . . .
In a genuine dialogue
each of the partners,
even when he stands
in opposition to the other,
heeds, affirms, and confirms
his opponent
as existing other.

        Martin Buber

A definite factor in getting a lie believed
is the size of the lie . . .
for the broad mass of the people,
in the primitive simplicity of its heart,
more readily falls victim to a big lie
than to a small one.

        Adolf Hitler

Once this separatism exists . . .
the ground is laid for all sorts
of psychological elaboration.
People who stay separate
have few channels of communication.
They easily exaggerate
the degree of difference between groups,
and readily misunderstand
the grounds for it.
And, perhaps most important of all,
the separateness may lead
to genuine conflicts of interests,
as well as to many imaginary conflicts.

        Gordon W. Allport

The problem of community,
which is the form of personal life,
is the one of deciding
on whose terms it shall be lived.
Simply to impose my terms
on the other person
is to deny his freedom and responsibility;
simply to accept his terms without demur
is to abandon my own.
In either case, there is no community
but a kind of fusion or absorption instead.
For community implies
a mutuality of distinct initiatives
that can never exist
as something settled once and for all,
but only as an ongoing project.

     Robert O. Johann

In another demonstration
of the power of stereotypes to affect our vision,
a number of Columbia and Barnard students
were shown thirty photographs
of pretty but unidentified girls,
and asked to rate each
in terms of "general liking,"
"intelligence," "beauty," and so on.

Two months later, the same group
were shown the same photographs,
this time with fictitious Irish, Italian, Jewish
and "American" names attached to the pictures.
Right away the ratings changed.
Faces which were now seen
as representing a national group
went down in looks
and still farther down in likability,
while the "American" girls suddenly
looked decidedly prettier and nicer.

                    Robert L. Heilbroner

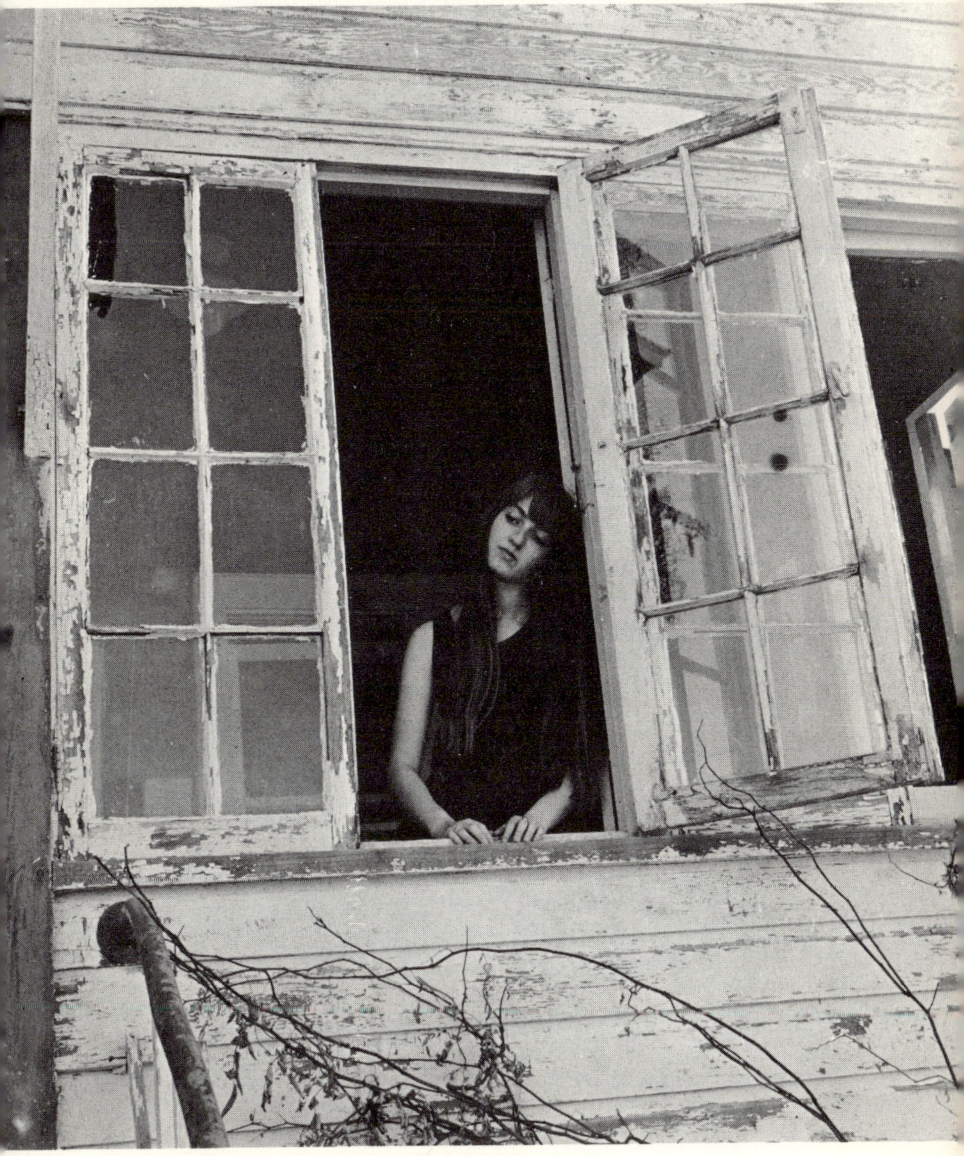

There is a whole civilization to be remade.

Albert Camus

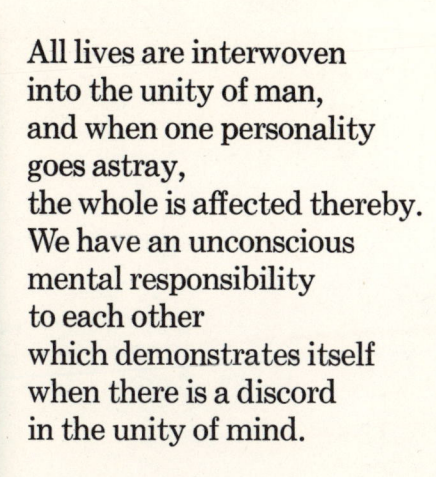

All lives are interwoven
into the unity of man,
and when one personality
goes astray,
the whole is affected thereby.
We have an unconscious
mental responsibility
to each other
which demonstrates itself
when there is a discord
in the unity of mind.

    David Kohn

The task is great
and full of responsibility.
It is nothing less
than that of leading the world
out of confusion
back to order.

    Richard Wilhelm

2
BLACK AND WHITE

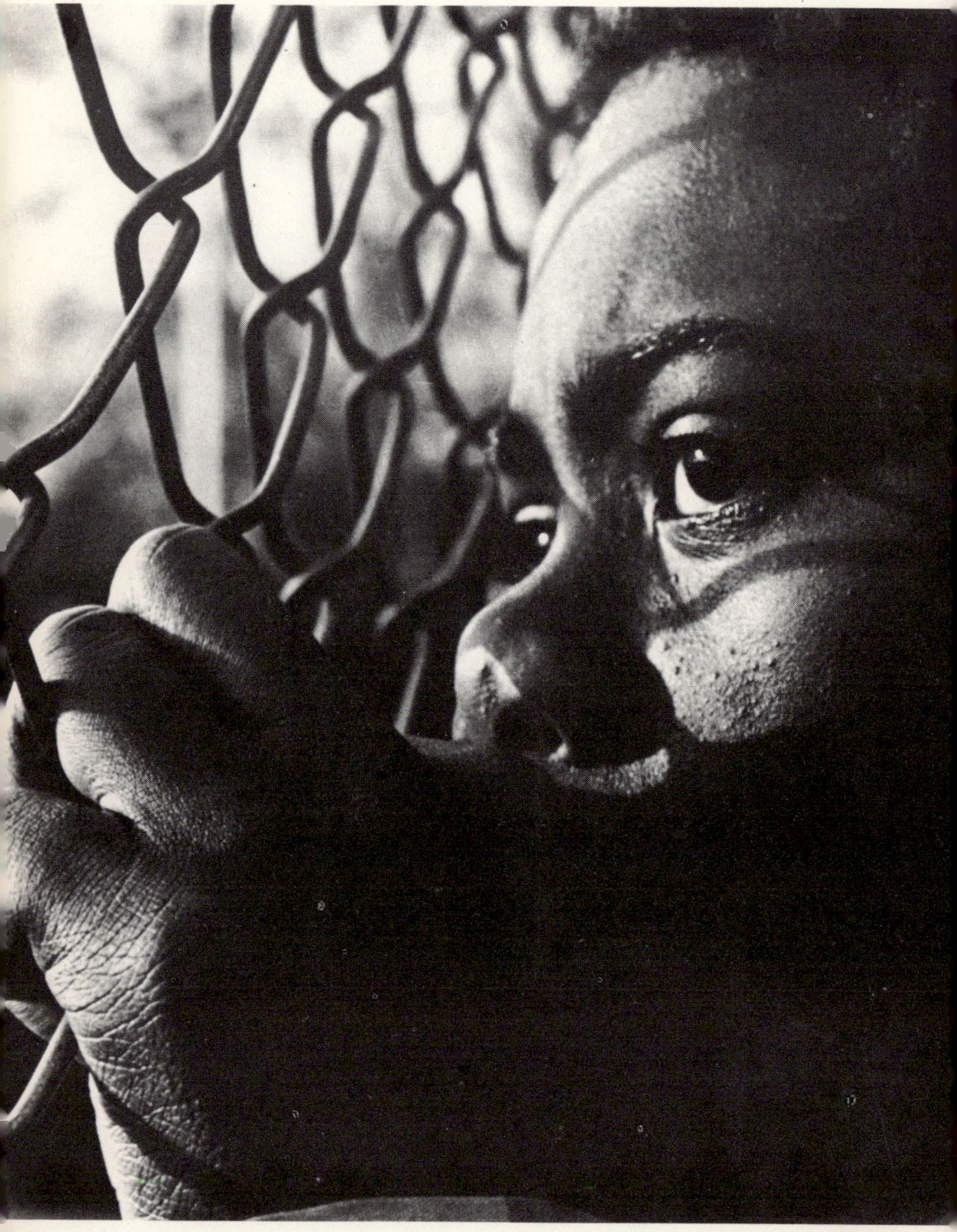

The Situation for Blacks

At home, sometimes they pass by
with pretended innocence and unconcern,
and then spit on the sidewalk behind us
to demonstrate their contempt;
or they scream "black nigger"
from the relative safety of passing cars.
I hated them for their open arrogance
and viciousness,
but I hated them even more
for their estimate of *us* —
their certainty that we were ignorant and bestial.
I could not see a Lindsay,
or a Bill, or a Bob among them;
they were white and therefore evil . . .
Do I hate as an act of self-defense
because I know that I'm hated?
Or do I hate because I'm evil, too?
Will I ever be entirely free of this hatred,
or has it grown in me for so long
that it is *me*, now and inseparable?
I'll find out soon. Yes, real soon . . .

                Thedford Slaughter

I'm terribly discouraged,
even frightened.
I have never seen the black
community
as completely disillusioned
and lacking in confidence . . .
I haven't lost the basic hope
that right will win out
but will it happen soon enough?

    Whitney Young

Everywhere I went
people called me brother . . .
"Welcome, American brother."
It was a good feeling for me,
to be in Africa.
To walk in a land
for the first time in your entire life
knowing within yourself
that your color
would not be held against you.
No black man ever knows this
in America.

    John O. Killens

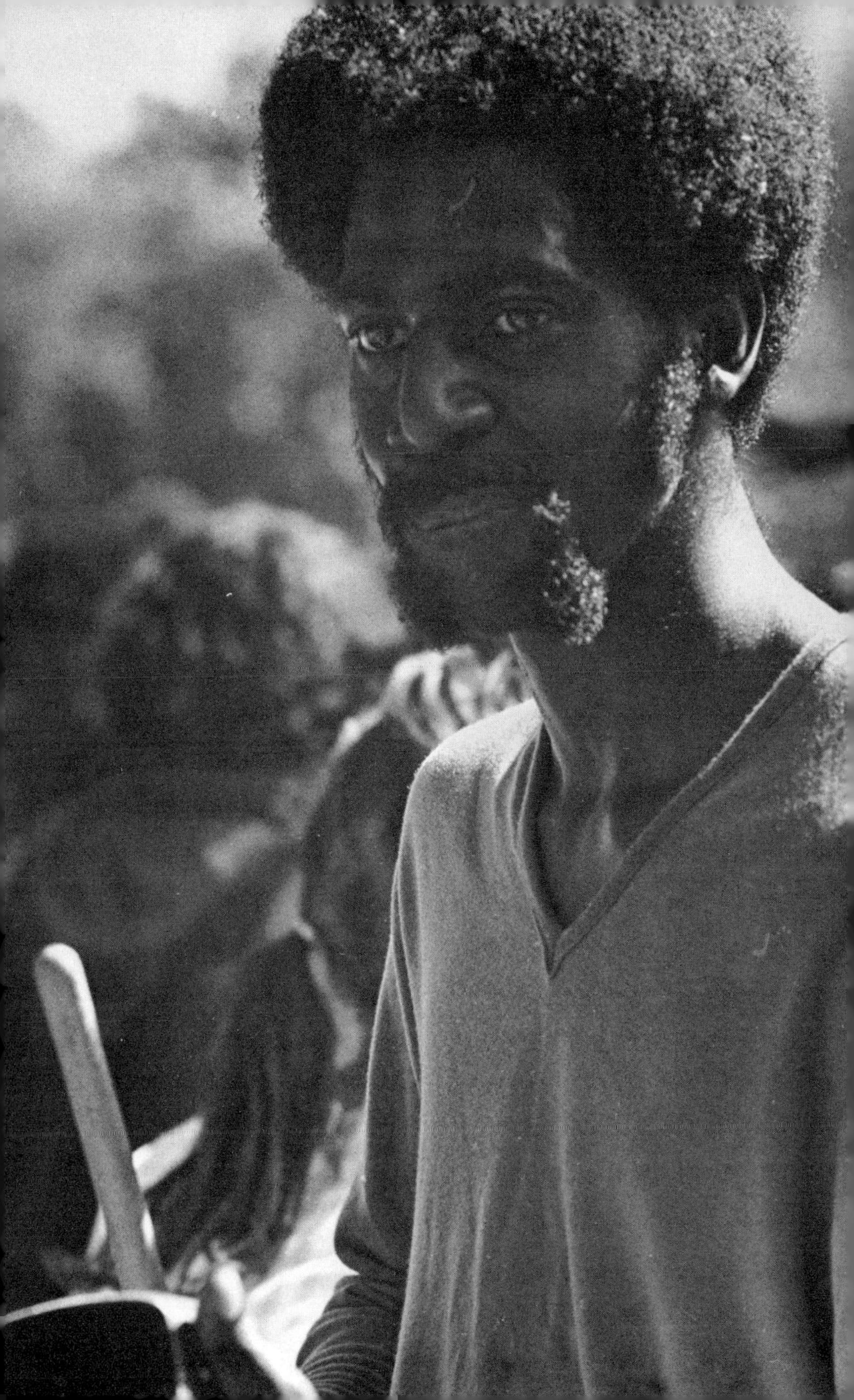

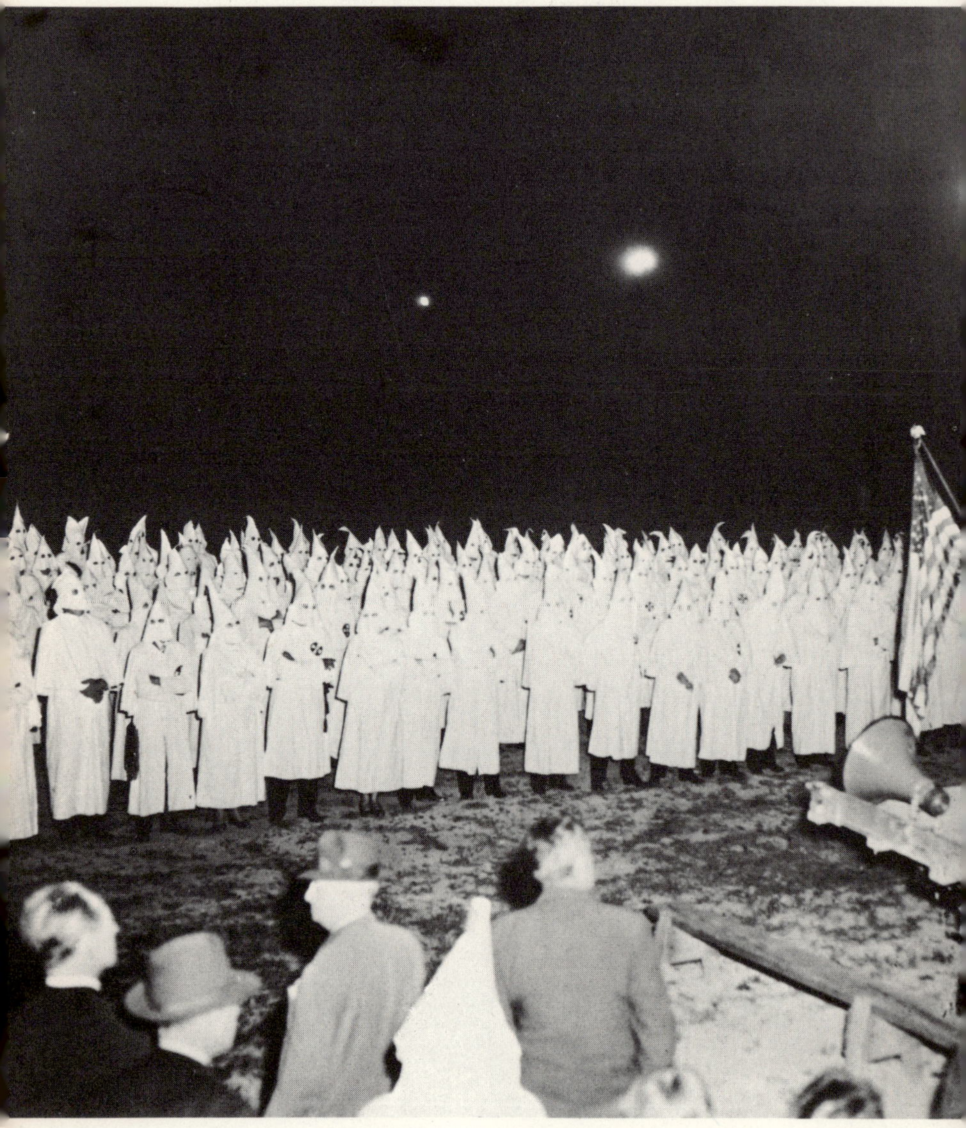

The whole question of race
is one that America would much rather
not face honestly and squarely.
To some, it is embarrassing;
to others, it is inconvenient;
to still others, it is confusing.
But for black Americans, to know it
and tell it like it is
and then to act on that knowledge
should be neither embarrassing
nor inconvenient nor confusing.
Those responses are luxuries
for people with time to spare,
who feel no particular sense of urgency
about the need to solve
certain serious social problems.
Black people in America have no time
to play nice, polite parlor games—
especially when the lives
of *their* children are at stake.

                Stokely Carmichael

Ask yourself what would happen
to your own personality
if you heard it said over and over again
that you were lazy,
a simple child of nature,
expected to steal,
and had inferior blood.
Suppose this opinion were forced on you
by the majority of your fellow citizens.
And suppose nothing that you could do
would change this opinion—
because you happened to have black skin.

Or suppose you heard daily
that you were expected to be
shrewd, sharp and successful in business,
that you were not wanted in clubs and hotels,
that you were expected to mingle
only with Jews
and then, if you did so,
were roundly blamed for it.
And suppose nothing that you could do
would change this opinion—
because you happened to be a Jew.

One's reputation,
whether false or true,
cannot be hammered into one's head
without doing something
to one's character.

      Gordon W. Allport

What atonement would
the God of Justice
demand for the robbery
of black people's labor,
their lives, their true identities,
their culture, their history...?

                Malcolm X

Radicals must be sufficiently
in tune to the society
to make short-term improvements
in order to keep up
the spirits and faith of the people.
If they do not, the people give up
and at that point the struggle ends.

                    Opara

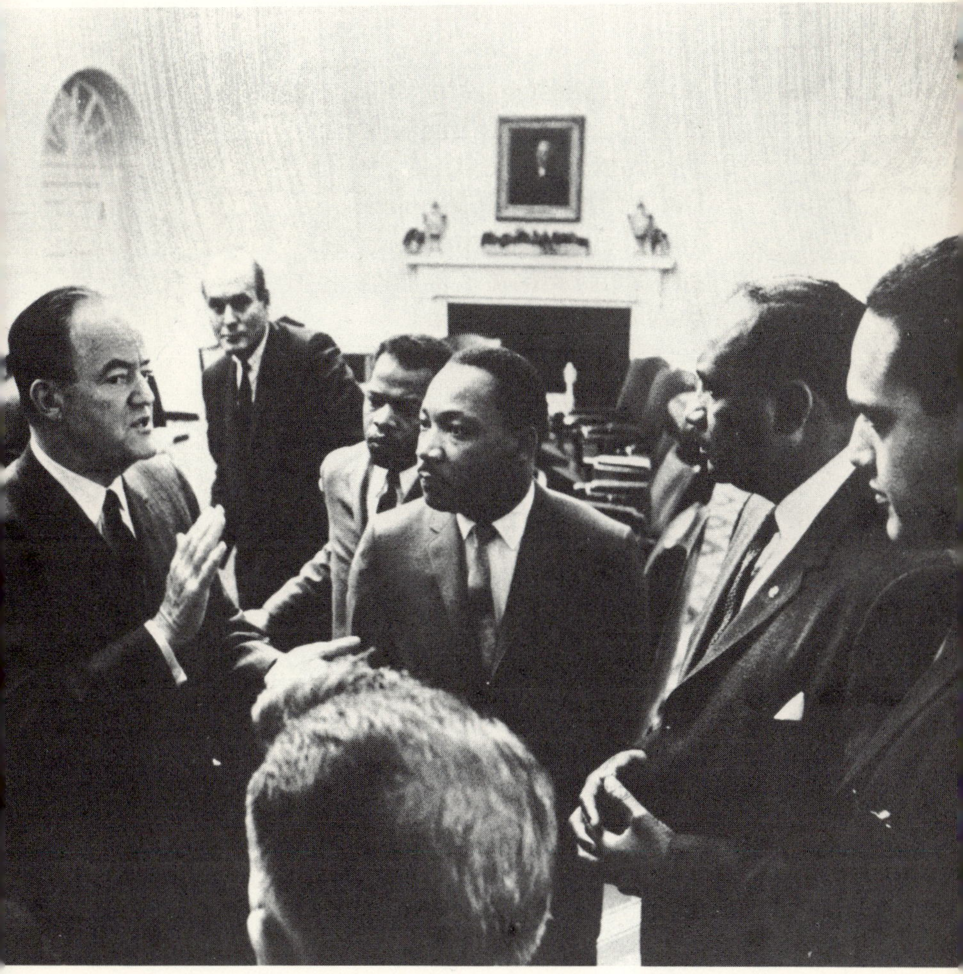

Race prejudice isn't
an old universal "instinct."
It is hardly a hundred years old.
Before that, people persecuted
Jews because of their religion—
not their "blood";
they enslaved Negroes
because they were pagans—
not for being black.

        Ruth Benedict
      and Gene Weltfish

In an age of decolonization,
it may be fruitful to regard
the problem of the American Negro
as a unique case of colonialism,
an instance of internal imperialism,
an underdeveloped people
in our very midst.

              I. F. Stone

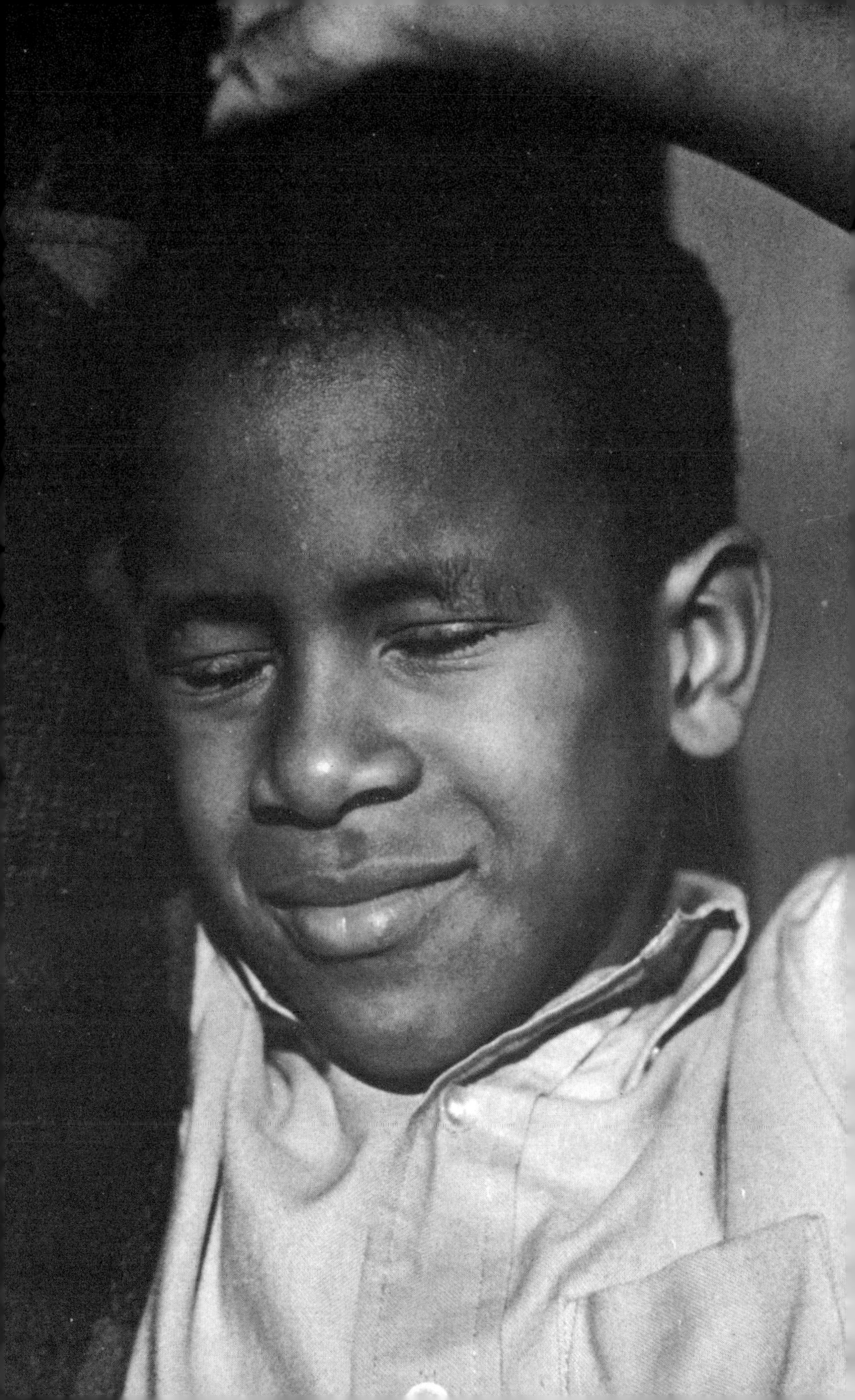

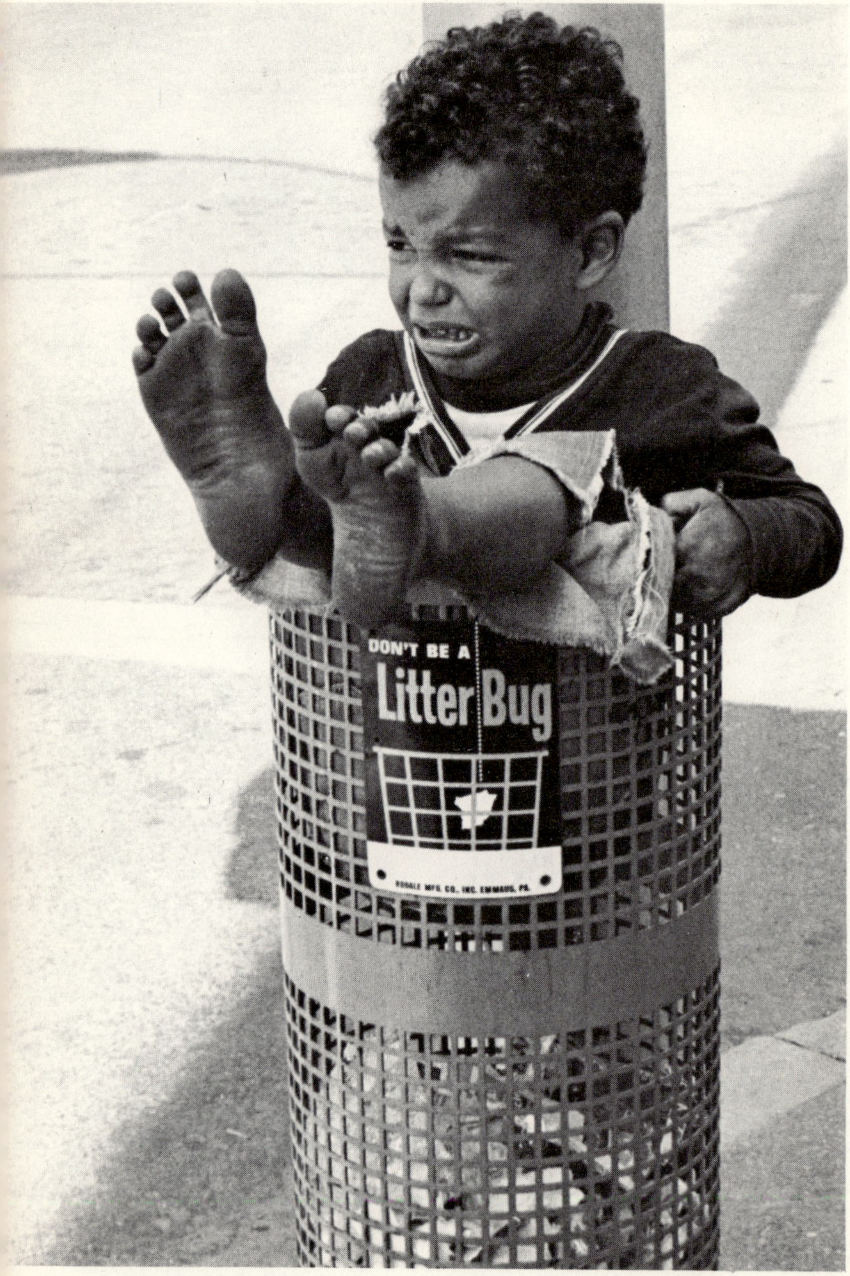
DON'T BE A
Litter Bug

Doing Something About the Crisis

Rebellion, in man,
is the refusal to be treated
as an object
and to be reduced
to simple historical terms.
It is the affirmation
of a nature
common to all men,
which eludes the world of power ...
Man, by rebelling
imposes in his turn
a limit to history
and at this limit
the promise of a value is born.

    Albert Camus

Those who profess to favor freedom
yet deprecate agitation,
are men who want crops
without plowing up the ground;
they want rain
without thunder and lightning.
They want the ocean
without the awful roar of its many waters.

    Frederick Douglass

I've been missing symbols
of black identity all my life.
I came to Radcliffe
with the fear that I still couldn't find them.
But then I went to Afro meetings.
There's a realization that you have
so much in common with other black students,
things that you can't share with whites.
It's just a beautiful feeling.

           Constance Hilliard

Pride of race and history
and the riddance of self-denunciation
are good and needed.
The thing to guard against is black arrogance.

           Roy Wilkins

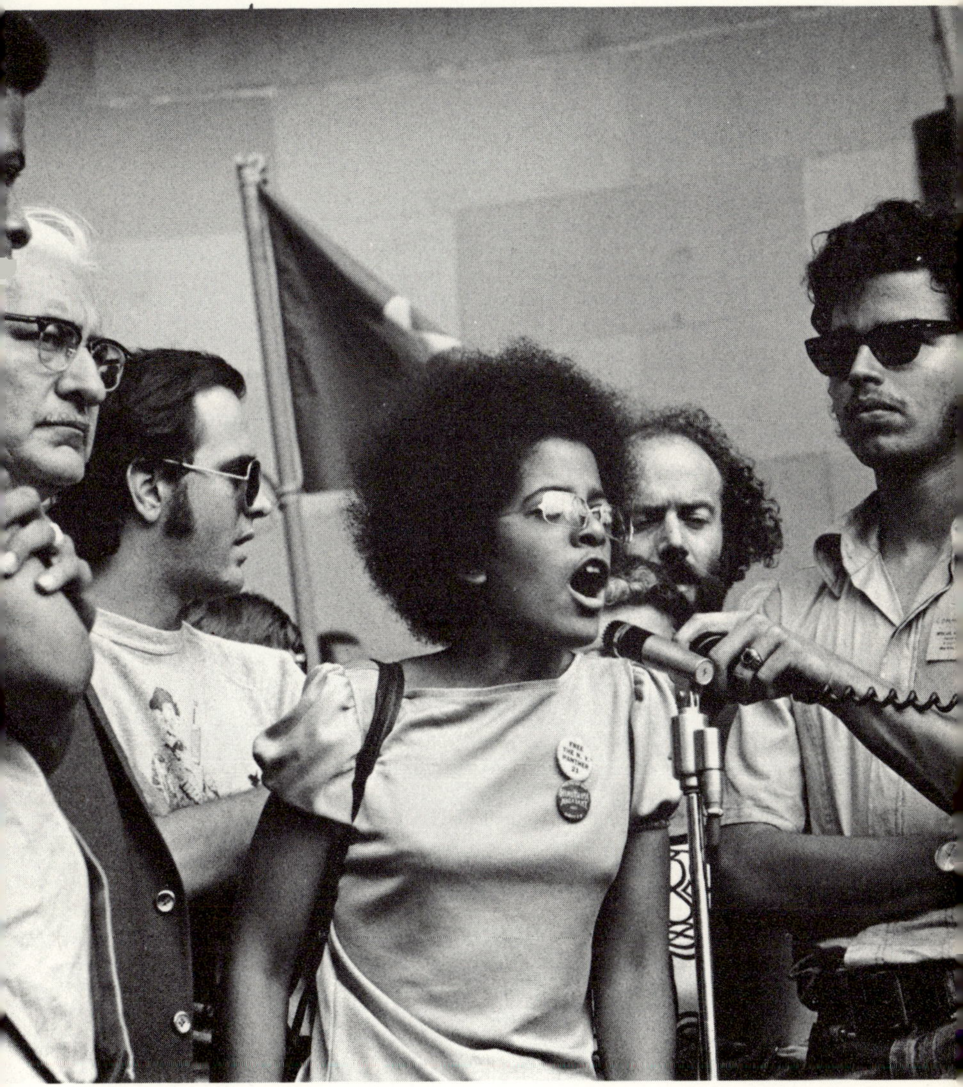

I have tried to stand between these two forces
saying that we need not follow
the "do-nothingism" of the complacent
or the hatred and despair
of the black nationalist.
There is the more excellent way
of love and nonviolent protest.
I'm grateful to God that,
through the Negro church,
the dimension of nonviolence
entered our struggle.
If this philosophy had not emerged
I am convinced that by now
many streets of the South
would be flowing with floods of blood.

    Dr. Martin Luther King

Up until now, one of the traditional complaints
of the black masses has been
of the treachery of black intellectuals...
there is a vast difference between Negroes
who are willing to go South
and all those generations
whose ambition was to flee the South.
A cycle has been completed.
The real work
for the liberation of black people
in America has begun.

                Eldridge Cleaver

The tragedy of race relations in the United States
is that there is no American Dilemma.
White Americans are not torn
and tortured by the conflict
between their devotion to the American creed
and their actual behavior.
They are upset by the current state
of race relations, to be sure.
But what troubles them
is not that justice is being denied,
but that their peace is being shattered
and their business interrupted.

       Charles Silberman

Lawyers and radicals are getting together.
It is an intimacy
with uncertain implications,
embarrassing some, delighting others,
unnerving a few.
Partly, that communion
reflects a growing radicalization
among lawyers and law students
and a shift to more political concerns.
Partly, it is imposed by the established order:
if you act like a nigger,
you'll be treated like one;
if you defend Black Panthers,
don't expect special dispensation
because you're a lawyer.

       Jonathan Black

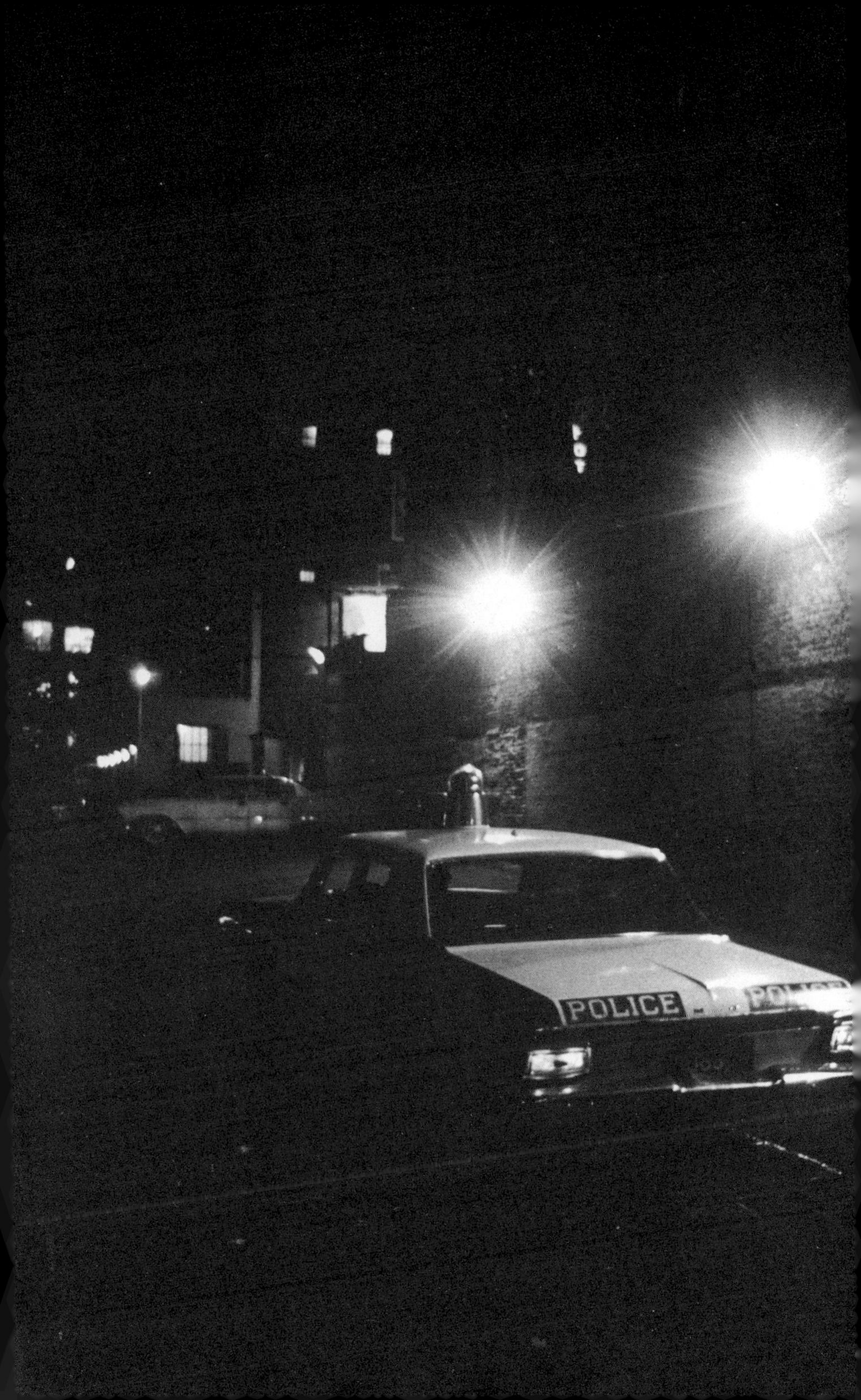
POLICE

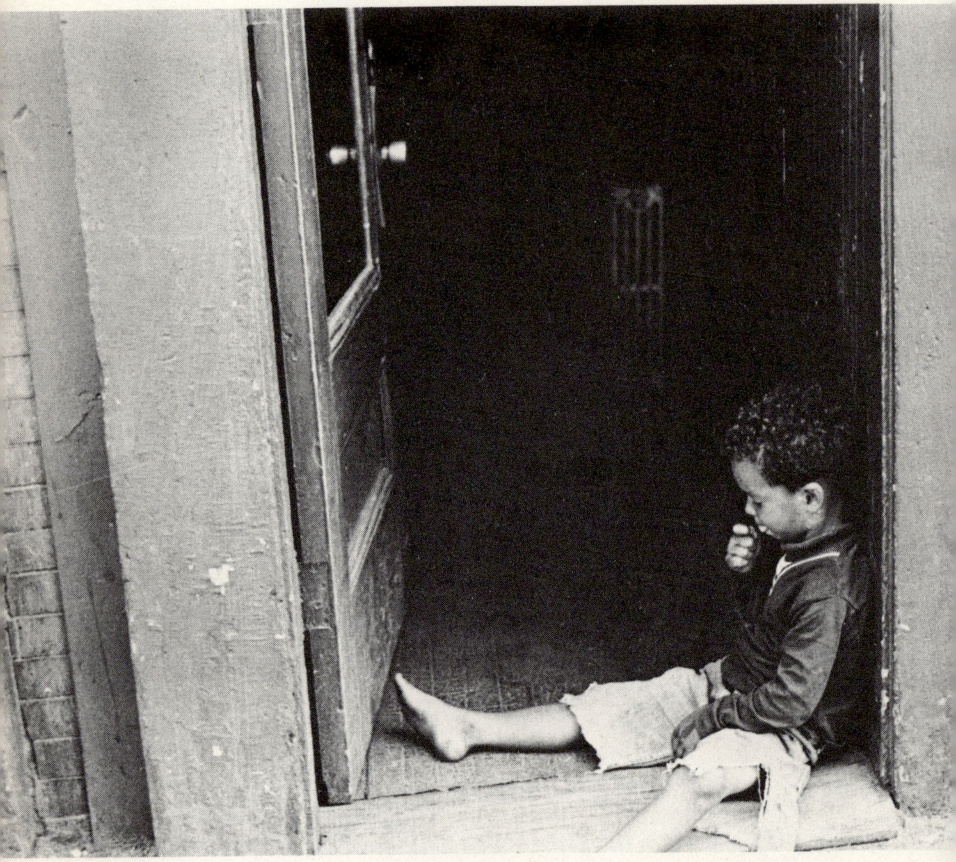

The Destiny of Brothers

Whenever someone with prejudices
speaks up against a group,
attacking Jews, Italians, or Negroes,
there is usually someone else
who comes up with a classic line of defense.
"Look at Einstein!"
"Look at Carver!"
"Look at Toscanini!"
"Of course Jews (or Italians, or Negroes)
must be all right."

They mean well, these defenders.
But their approach is wrong.
Their approach is even bad.
What a minority group wants
is not the right to have
geniuses among them,
but the right to have fools and scoundrels—
without being condemned as a group.
Every group has about the same
proportion of wrongdoers.
But when wrongdoers belong to a minority
their number is magnified
in the minds of other people.
Minorities would gladly give up
the reflected glory of their great men,
if only the world didn't burden them
with the ignominy of their scoundrels.
Both types belong to mankind
as a whole, and mankind as a whole
may share the sorrow as well as the honor.

      Libby Benedict

I know there is something there
Under the black skin,
Behind the Jewish nose,
I cannot now know;
That was never instilled
In that time of becoming
Whatever it is I have become;
That feeling, that just possible
Sneaky suspicion about all this
Equality talk and am I really then?
Or something less than . . . ?

My unknowing is all I can offer,
My knowing the unknowing,
And the crying inside
Wanting it not to be so for you,
That suspicion
That sneaks into tight places.

                Ione Hill

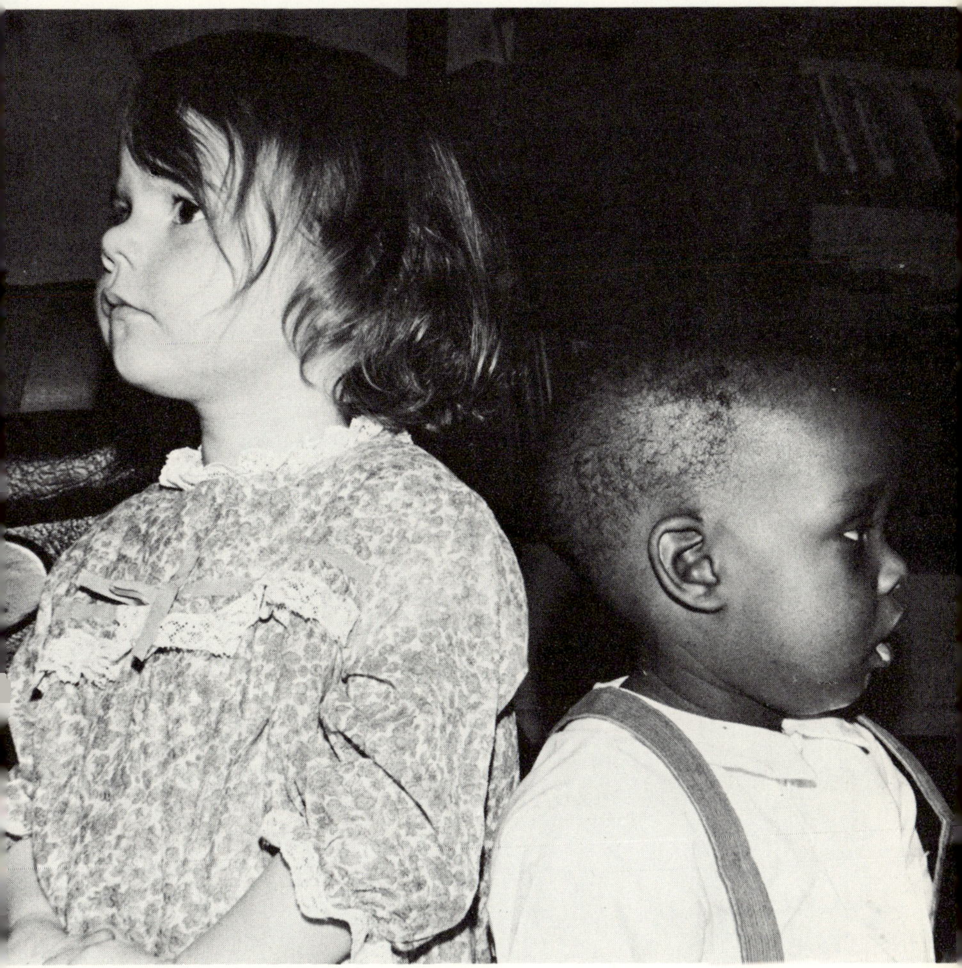

No longer through exclusion
but only inclusion
can the kingdom be established.
When it no longer horrifies you
and no longer disgusts you,
when you redeem the crowd into men
and strike even the heart
of the crude, the greedy, the stingy
with your love,
then and then alone
is there present,
in the midst of the end,
the new beginning.

    Martin Buber

There is a destiny that makes us brothers;
None goes his way alone;
All that we send into the lives of others
Comes back into our own.

        Edwin Markham

3

LET
MY
PEOPLE
GO

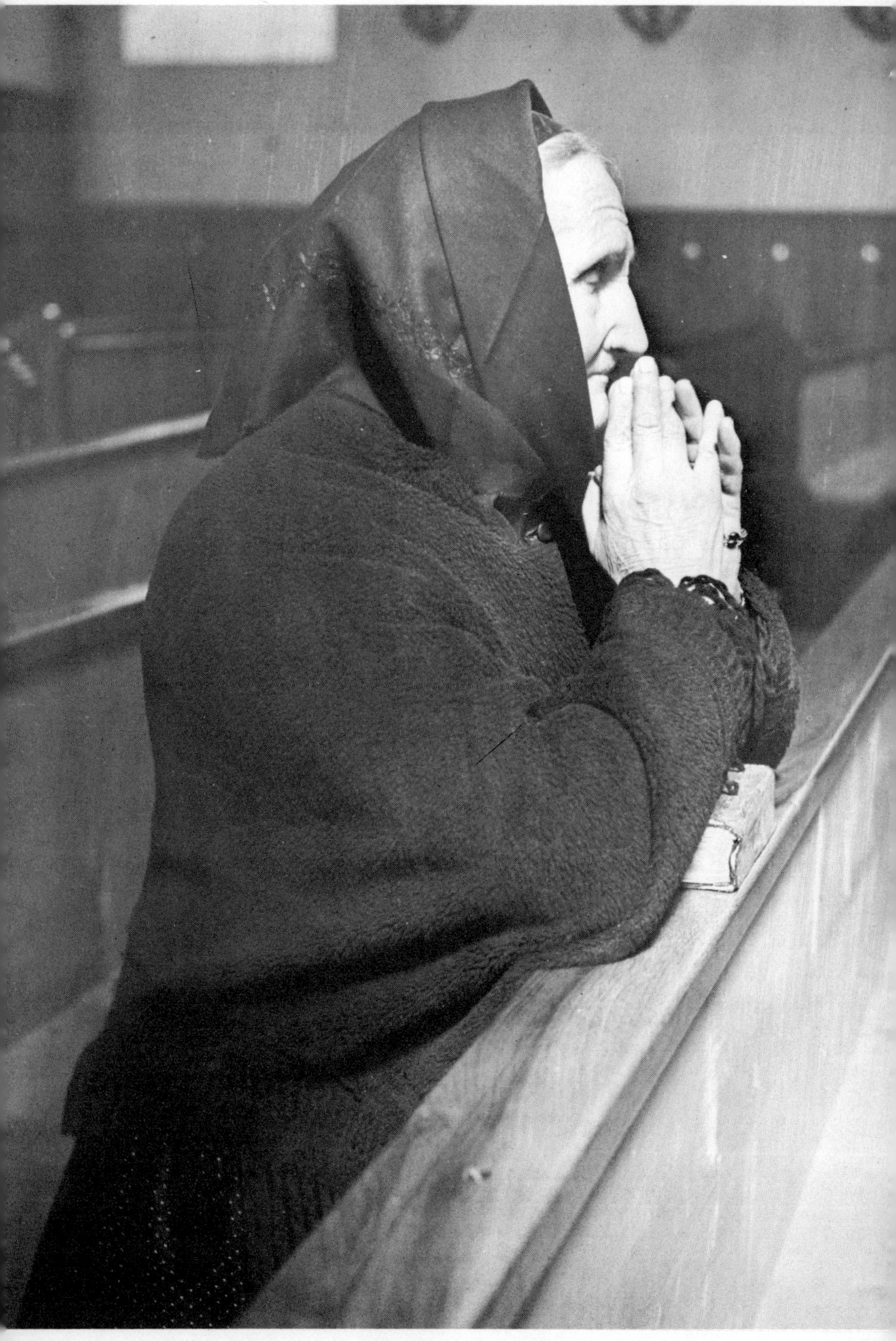

The Religious Condition

Knowledge of ourselves teaches us
whence we come, where we are
and whither we are going.
We come from God
and we are in exile;
and it is because our potency
of affection tends towards God
that we are aware of this state of exile.

      John Ruysbroeck

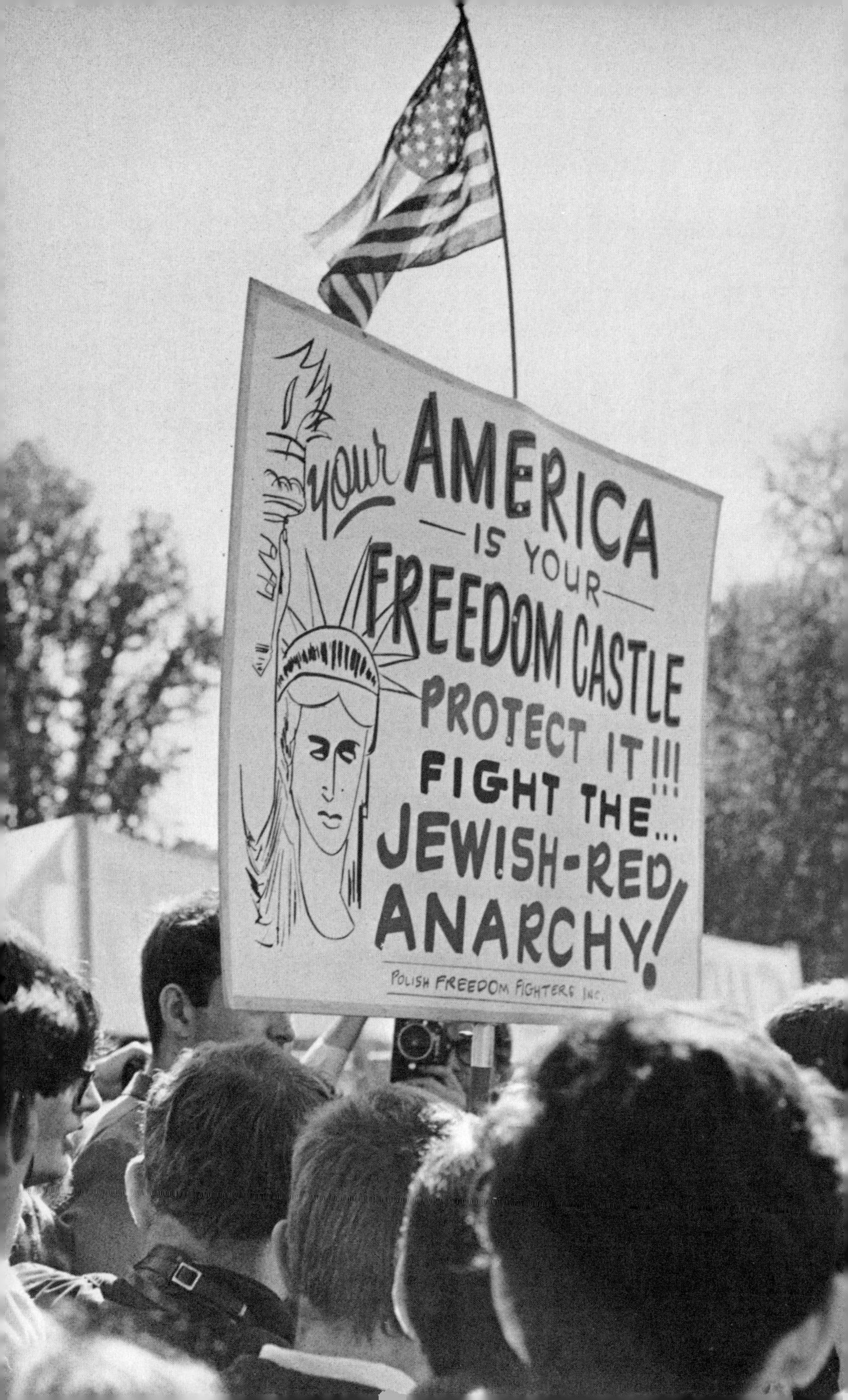

your AMERICA
IS YOUR
FREEDOM CASTLE
PROTECT IT!!!
FIGHT THE...
JEWISH-RED
ANARCHY!
POLISH FREEDOM FIGHTERS INC.

Faith will move a mountain . . .
It hasn't dislodged prejudice.
But I think education could . . .

    Heywood Broun

Man is made by his belief.
As he believes, so he is.

    Bhagavad Gita

In history God has often encountered
moral intransigence that would budge
before nothing less than violence.
In these cases, chronicled
by Jeremiah and Ezekiel,
God did not hesitate
to call men to destroy
existing institutions,
even the most sacred of institutions,
his own temple.

    Paul J. Weber

The death of a culture begins
when its normative institutions
fail to communicate ideals
in ways that remain
inwardly compelling,
first of all
to the cultural elites themselves.

    Philip Rieff

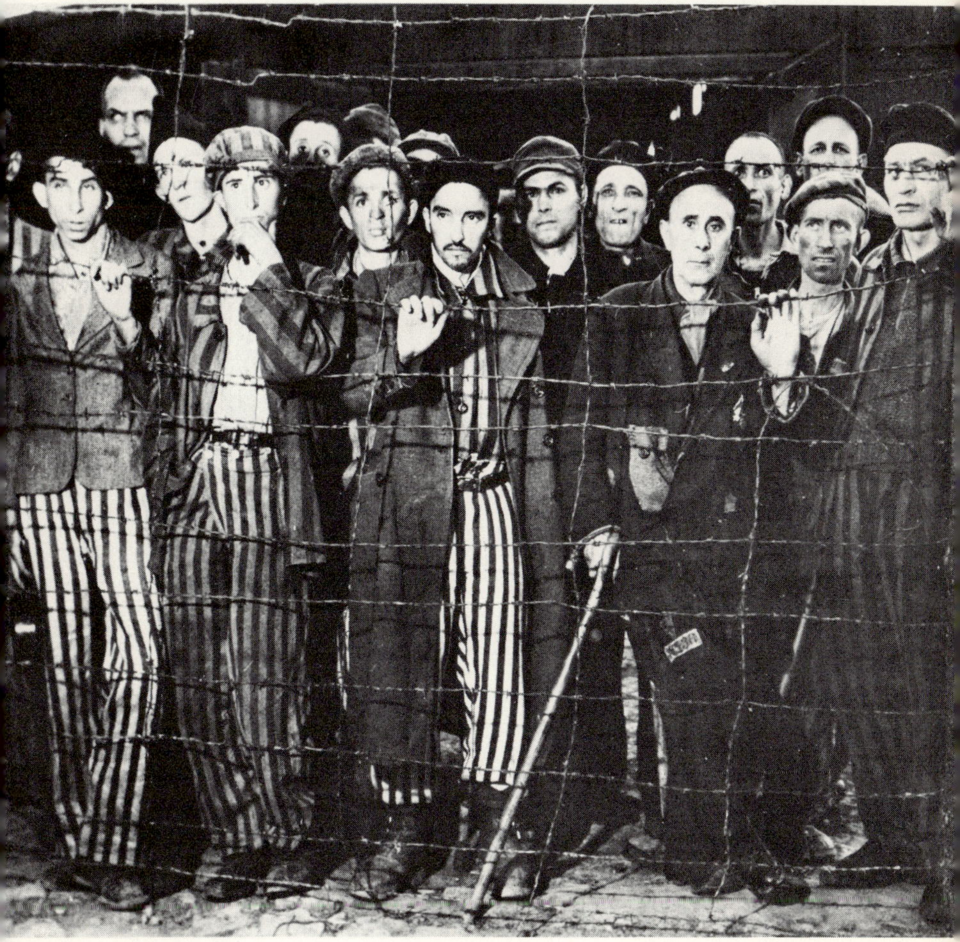

Congress shall make no laws
respecting an establishment of religion,
or prohibiting the free exercise thereof . . .

    Bill of Rights

We would have inward peace,
Yet will not look within;
We would have misery cease,
Yet will not cease from sin.

    Matthew Arnold

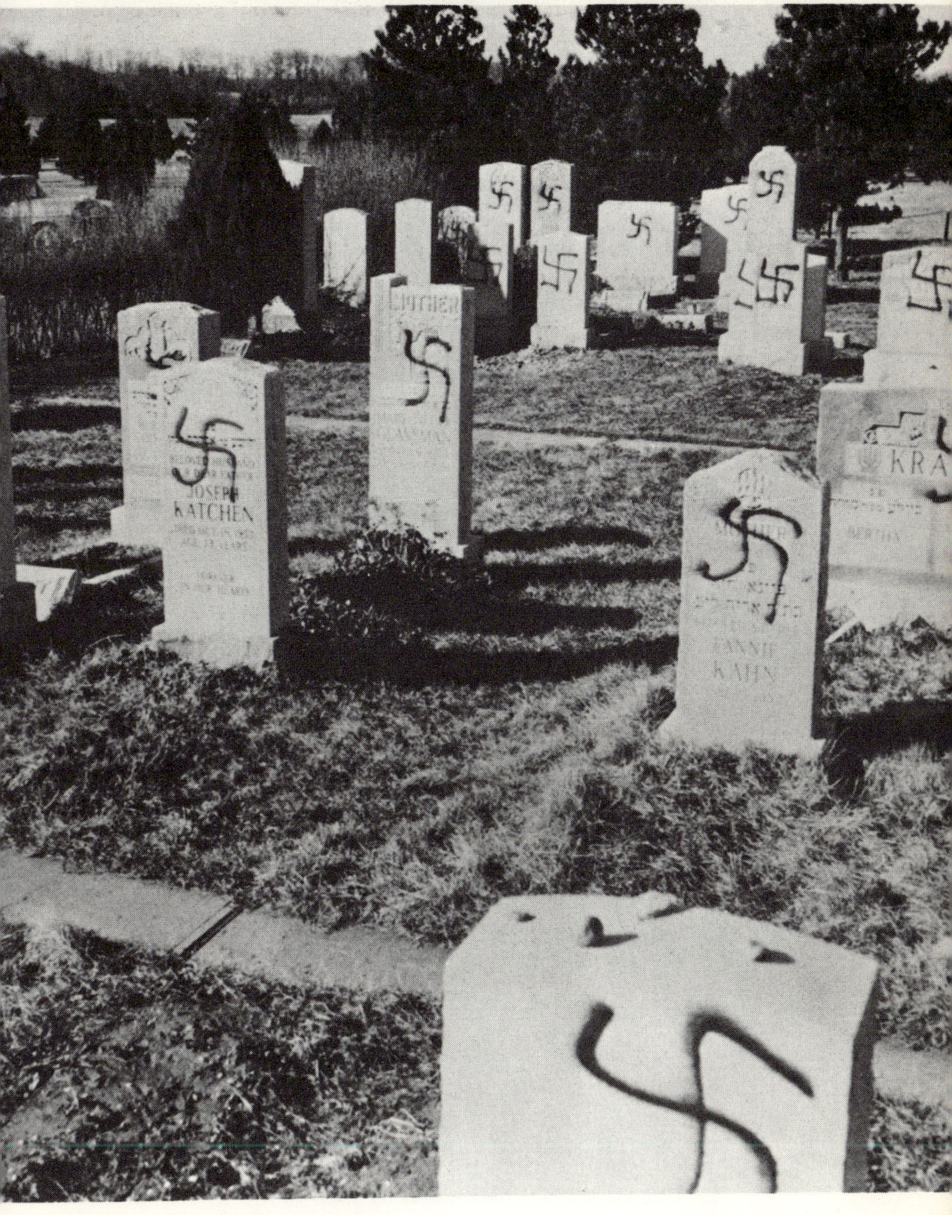
JOSEPH
KATCHEN
KRA

It is very nice to think
The world is full of meat and drink,
With little children saying grace
In every Christian kind of place.

    Robert Louis Stevenson

The Case of Anti-Semitism

My Jews are a valuable hostage,
given to me by the democracies.
Anti-Semitic propaganda in all countries
is an indispensable medium
for the extension of our political campaign.
You will see how little time we shall need
in order to upset the ideas . . . of the whole world,
simply and purely by attacking Judaism.

                    Adolf Hitler

I discovered in talking with Christians and Jews
that although Jews were acutely aware
of the extent and intensity of anti-Semitism,
Christians were almost totally ignorant of it.
The infamous pages of history
which Jews have memorized
have been torn, so to speak,
out of our Christian history books.
I am convinced that the more rapidly
Christians learn the facts about anti-Semitism...
the more rapidly the disease will be cured.

                    Edward H. Flannery

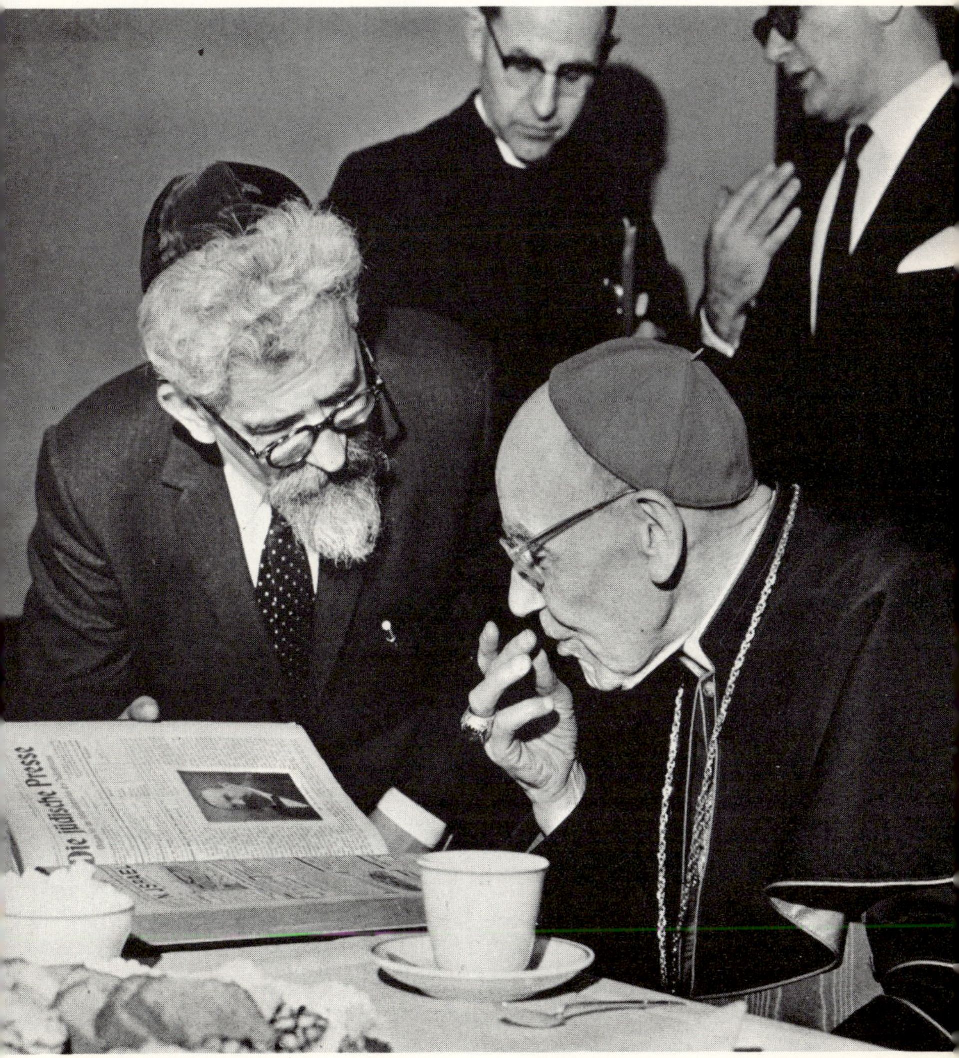
Die jüdische Presse

Everything we are as Jews,
including our drive
occasionally to grope
beyond traditional bounds,
comes directly from the Bible.
In size we are nothing as a people
and never have been.
Had we not been children of the Book,
who would have heard of us?
We should be lucky to occupy
a mere footnote in history.
As things stand, a large part
of history is our doing.
We have never been far removed
from the mainstream,
often unhappily so and at peril.

    David Ben-Gurion

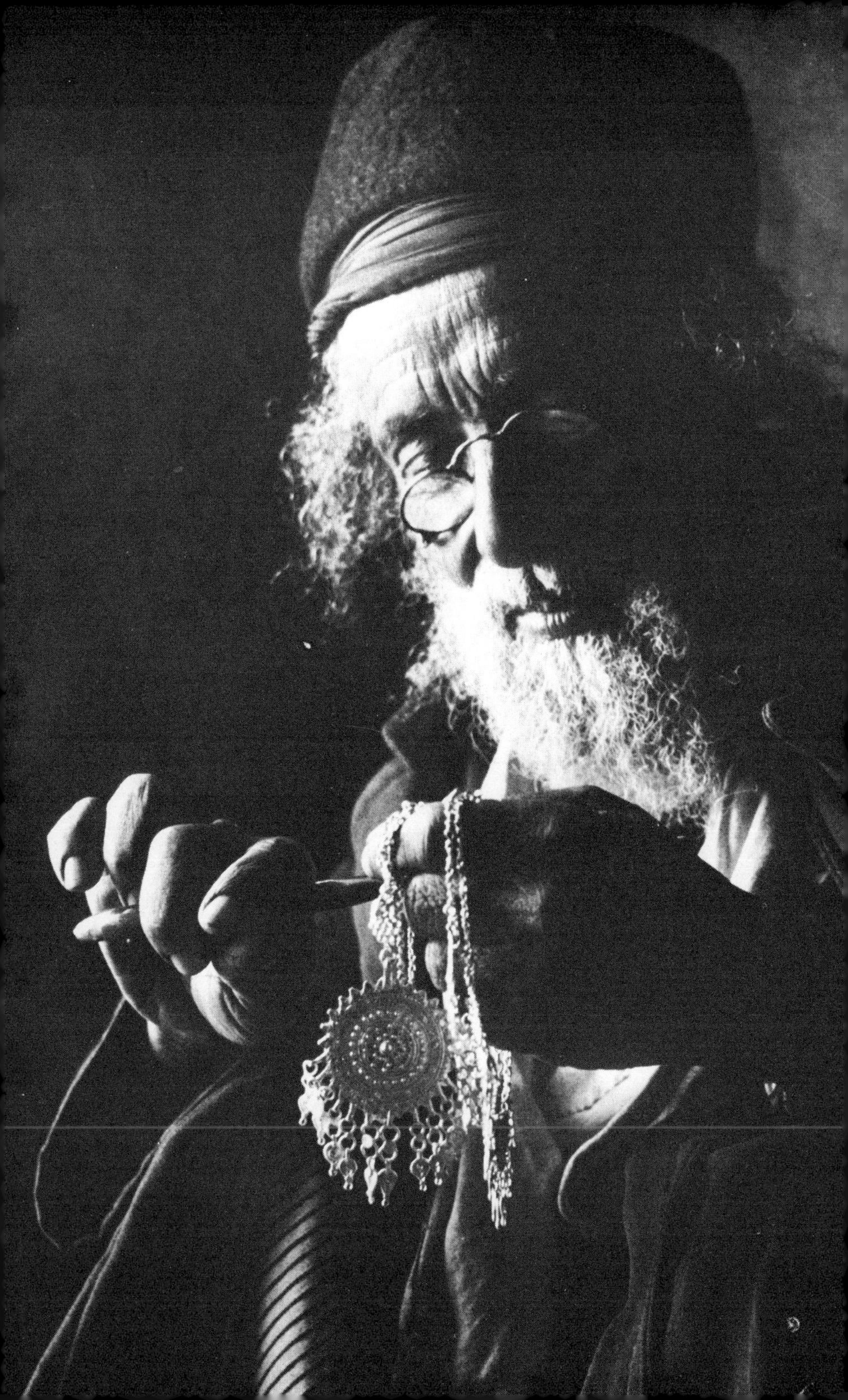

HOTEL COLUMBIA
and Cottages

W. HARVEY JONES
Owner and Manager

*An Elegantly Appointed Modern Hostelry
Catering to the Most Exclusive Patronage*

*We positively do not solicit
the patronage of Hebrews*

ASBURY PARK, N. J.

Young Jewish executives
are still finding the executive club
to be a decided hangup
on their way to jobs
that match their abilities.
Although some are suddenly
opening up to men at the top,
and although change is in the air,
executive social clubs are still very much
the last bastion of anti-Semitism in business.

                         Craig Vetter

To all our Jewish Friends:

On the occasion of this tribute from Jewish leaders of the United States the Catholic Bishops of this country warmly reaffirm the Declaration of the Fathers of Vatican Council II that Christians and Jews are all children of God, all sharing "His providence, His manifestations of goodness, His saving design."

We recall with deep satisfaction the patient and friendly dialogue in which so many representatives of the Jewish faith participated during the Council. These personal conversations, extending over a four year period, enriched the Church's awareness of the "spiritual patrimony common to Christians and Jews," the common heritage of salvation in the covenant made between God and Abraham and his descendants.

In this exchange of tributes we Catholic people of the United States salute our Jewish brothers anew, and pledge ourselves to continue fostering stronger and more extensive bonds of mutual understanding, of respect and of cooperation. It is our prayer that this occasion may inspire further confidence that men of all faiths can aid one another in attaining peace and live as brothers.

Washington, District of Columbia
November 13, 1966

PRESENTED TO
THE AMERICAN JEWISH COMMITTEE
BY
THE CATHOLIC BISHOPS
OF THE UNITED STATES

If we want to cure men
of the spiritual corruption
of racism and anti-Semitism
we must ever remind them
that they were born for freedom
and that they are equal before the law,
and that they receive from natural law
inviolable rights and infrangible duties.
And let us ever remind them
that God is truth and love,
let us remind them of the unity of mankind
and of the spiritual dignity
of the human person,
of the sovereign law of brotherly love,
of all that the gospel has taught us,
not only for eternal life,
but also for the earthly life
of individuals and peoples.

                Jacques Maritain

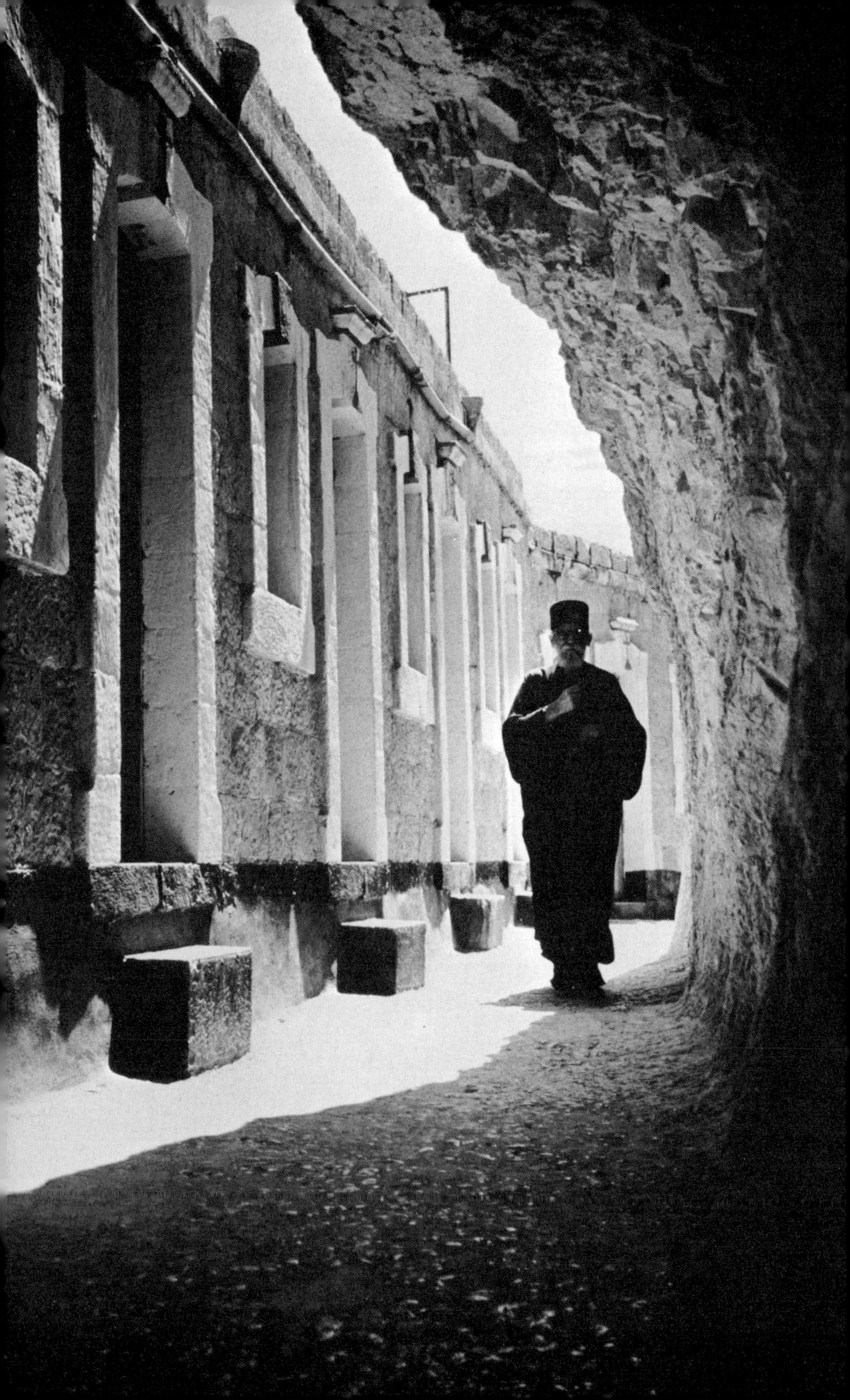

Religious Response to Religious Prejudice

Having purified your souls
by your obedience to the truth
for a sincere love of the brethren,
love one another earnestly from the heart.
You have been born anew,
not of perishable seed but of imperishable,
through the living and abiding word of God.

                        1 Peter 1:22—23

For he is our peace,
who has made us both one,
and has broken down
the dividing wall
of hostility.

       Ephesians 2:14

Modern man sees his destinies in the world;
he has decided to take his fate
into his own hands.
Even the religious person
will hardly deny that this is
the real task that God has set
for man in this life:
to make use of all his faculties
and so to become a real man;
to build a world of truthfulness,
of justice and morality
in which the diverse nations
may co-operate with all their strength
towards the realization
of their common ideals,
so as to make the earth
a more perfect dwelling place
for humanity.

      Erich Frank

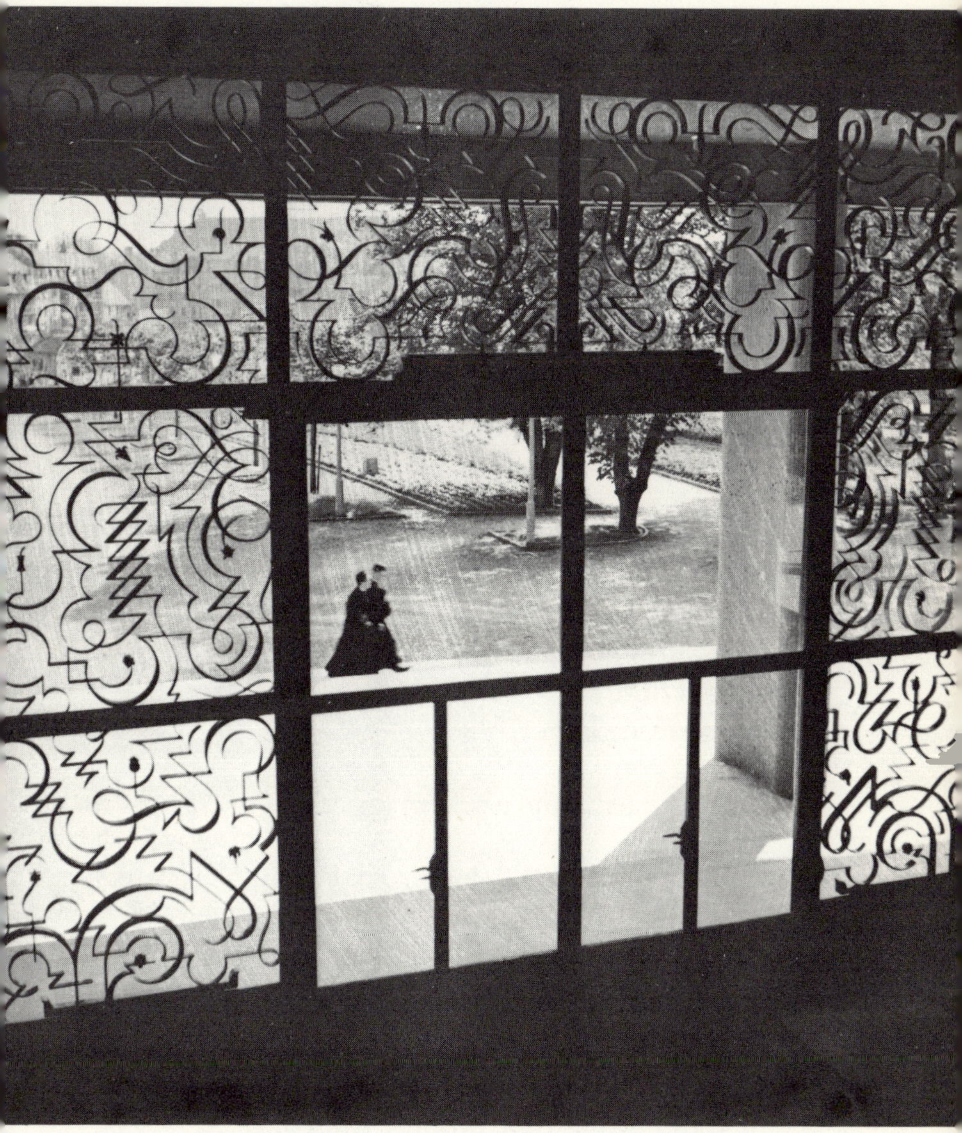

I sought to hear the voice of God,
    And climbed the topmost steeple.
But God declared: "Go down again,
    I dwell among the people."

        Louis I. Newman

The ideal life is in our blood
and never will be still.
Sad will be the day for any man
when he becomes contented
with the thoughts he is thinking
and the deeds he is doing,—
where there is not forever beating
at the doors of his soul
some great desire
to do something larger,
which he knows
that he was meant and made to do.

        Phillips Brooks

The truth indeed has never been preached by the Buddha,
seeing that one has to realize it within oneself.

        Sutralamkara

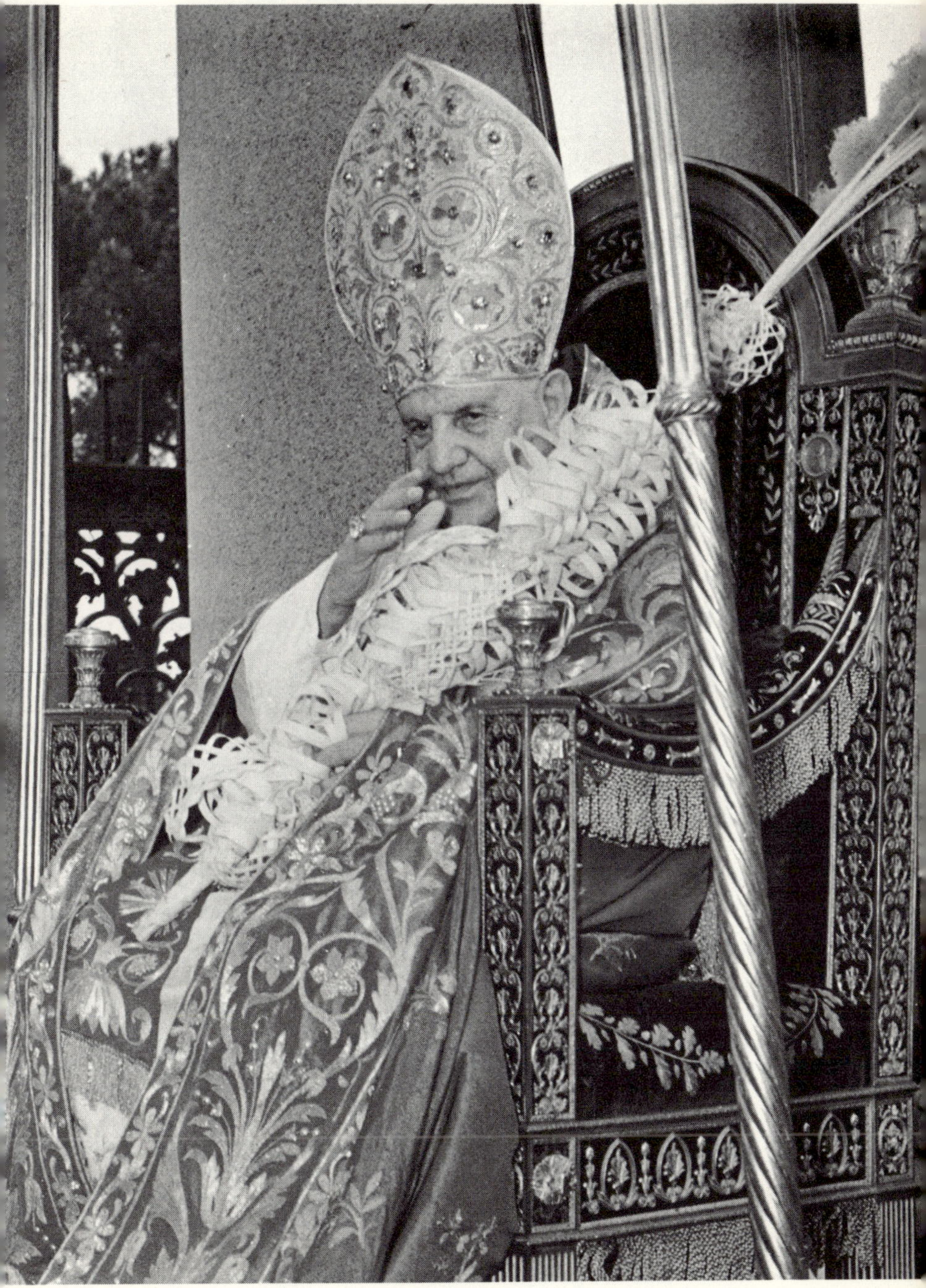

4

A WOMAN'S PLACE

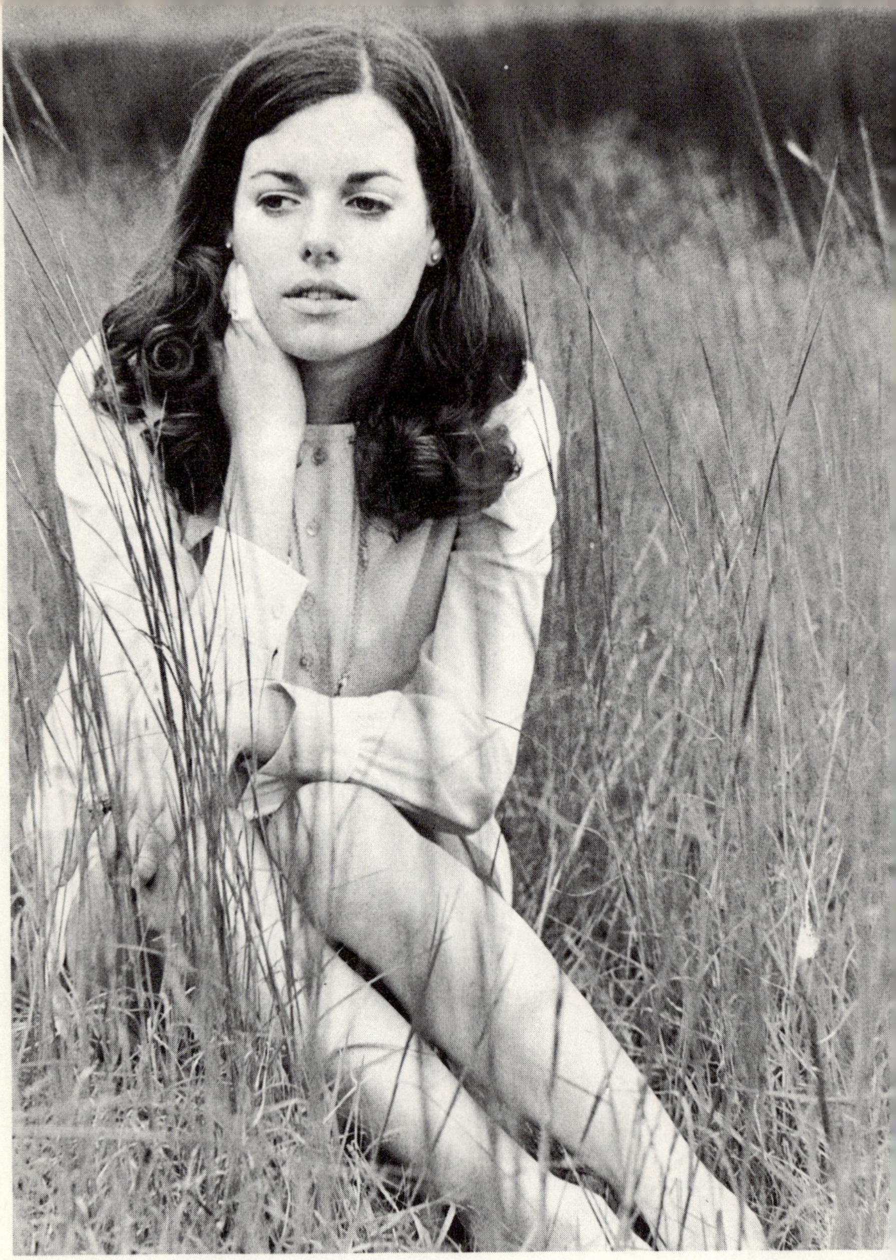

Freud as Public Enemy

The whole education of women
ought to be relative to men.
To please them,
to be useful to them,
to make themselves loved
and honored by them,
to educate them when young,
to care for them when grown,
to counsel them,
to make life sweet
and agreeable to them—
these are the duties of women
at all times,
and what should be taught them
from their infancy.

    Jean-Jacques Rousseau

As we learn from psychoanalytic work,
women regard themselves as wronged
    from infancy,
as undeservedly cut short and set back;
and the embitterment of so many daughters
    against their mothers
derives, in the last analysis,
from the reproach against her
of having brought them into the world
as women instead of men.

    Sigmund Freud

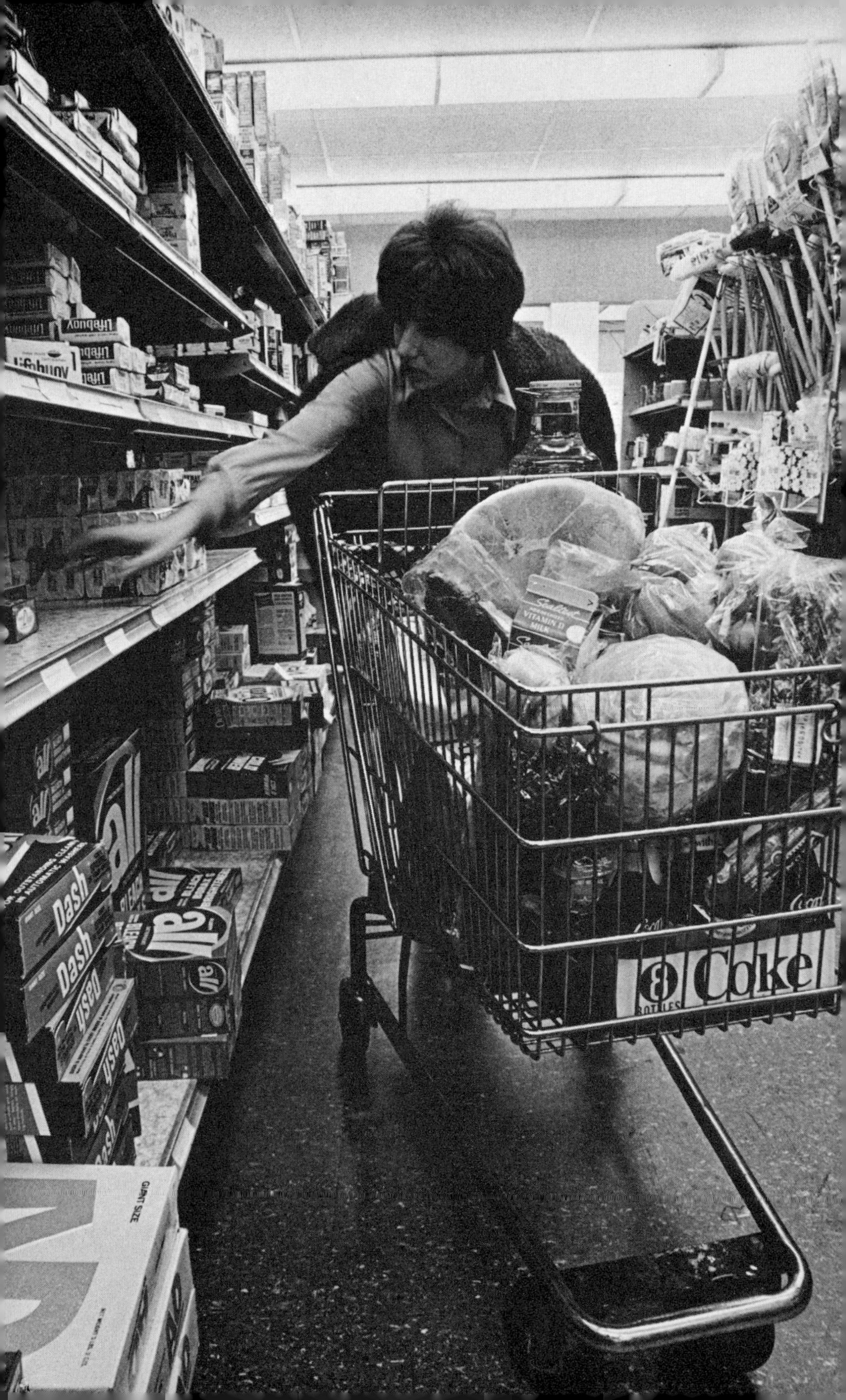
Lifebuoy
Dash
all
8
BOTTLES
Coke

As matters now stand,
women occupy a place in this country
that is, not accidentally,
tailored to the needs of men
in an ever-expanding profit economy.
Socially, women are child bearers
and homemakers,
freeing men to pursue success
and self-definition
in the larger world outside the home.

        Karen Durgin

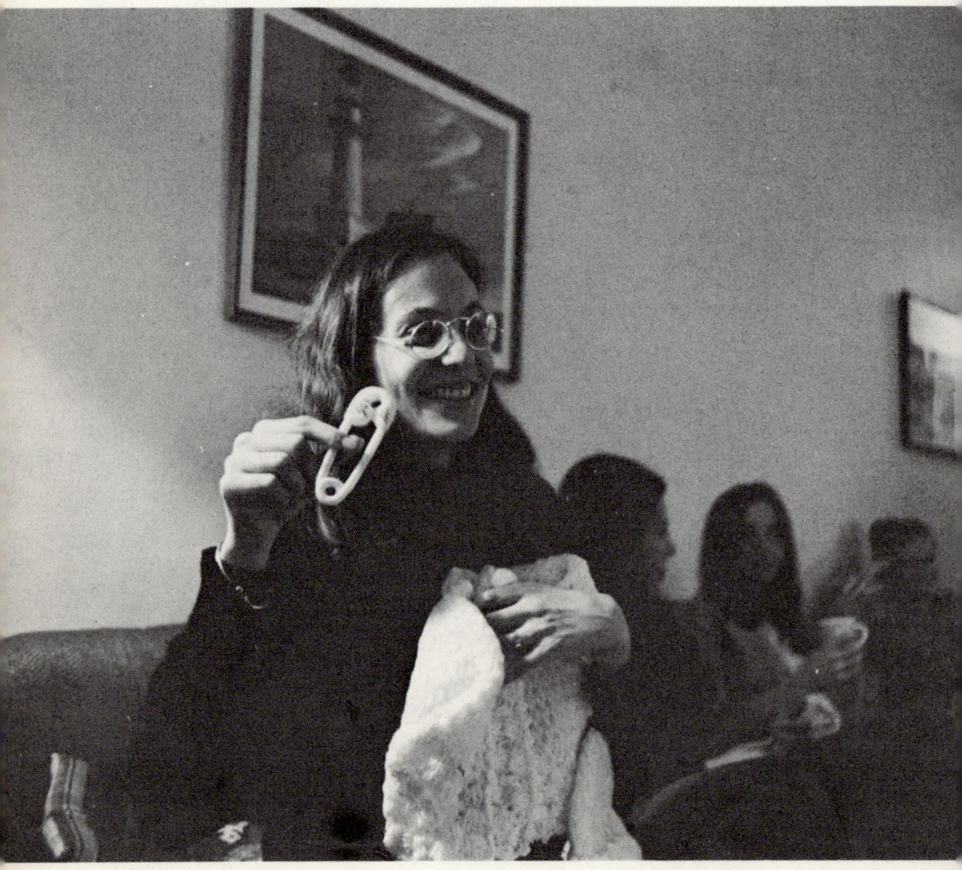

Too often being a woman in America
implies accepting the role
of potholder maker,
Christmas-card addresser
and Band-Aid dispenser.
It may even mean,
against all one's best intentions,
that one has nothing interesting
to say to the husband
who returns home each evening.

                Roberta Madden

Our goal is to make women
aware of their power,
and the fact that they can use this power
to make changes in the world.

And if changes aren't made
I'm afraid that what could happen with women
might make the race riots in Detroit
look like child's play.

                          Betty Friedan

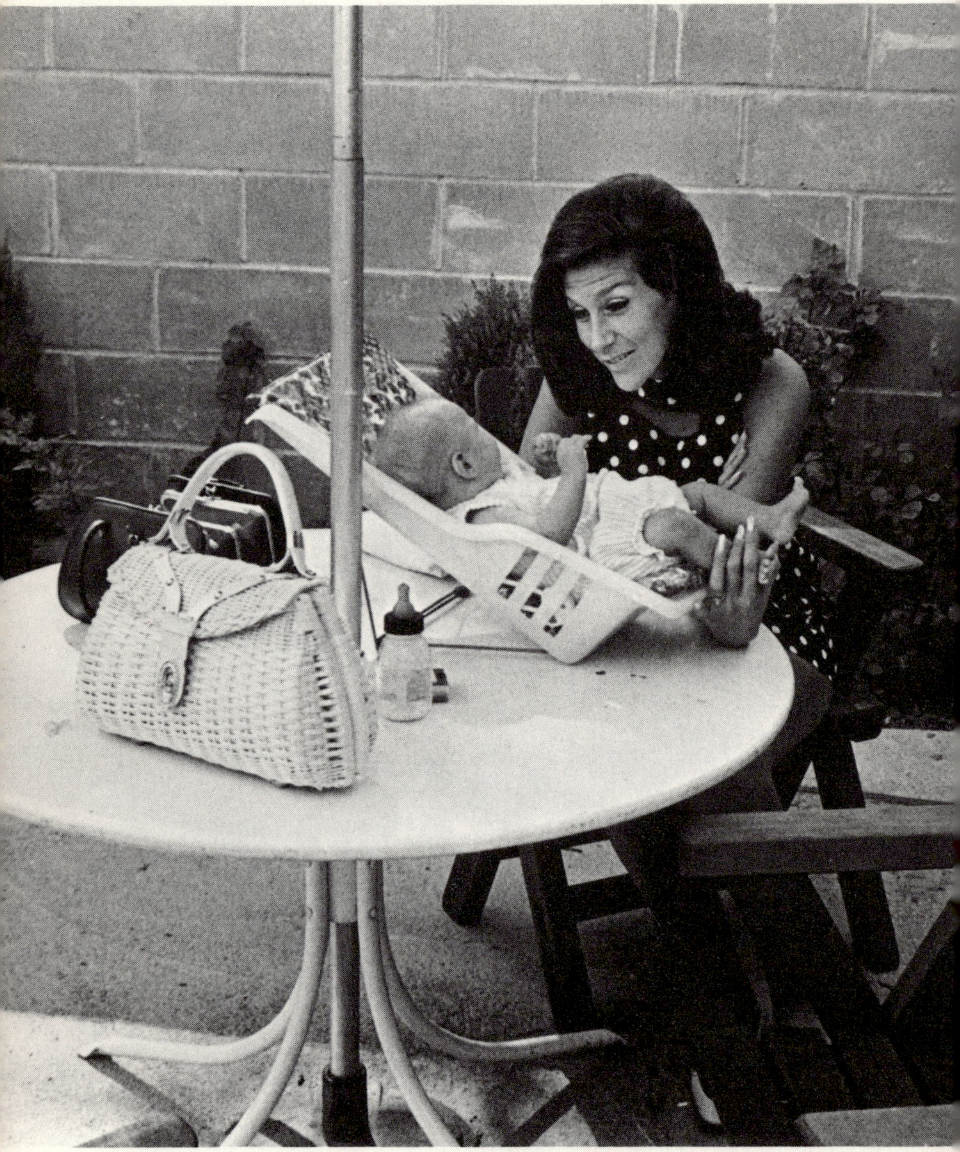

The Least Finished Revolution

While I have no desire to abandon
my husband and children
or unfurl my bra in public protest,
I do have an intense need
to survive as an individual.
I need recognition
as an intelligent woman
with ideas and goals,
rather than as a tired wife and mother
smothered by the demands
of her family.

        Cheryl Henderson

While we realize
that the liberation of women
will ultimately mean
the liberation of men
from the destructive role
as oppressor,
we have no illusion
that men will welcome
this liberation
without a struggle...

    Manifesto of the New York
    Radical Feminists

It's time a man
spoke up for Women's Lib,
not just because it's here to stay
but because it's right.
It's time for women to raise hell
and for men to help them do it.
The very nature of the movement
makes it a men's liberation as well—
we'll all be better for it.

        P. B. Frank

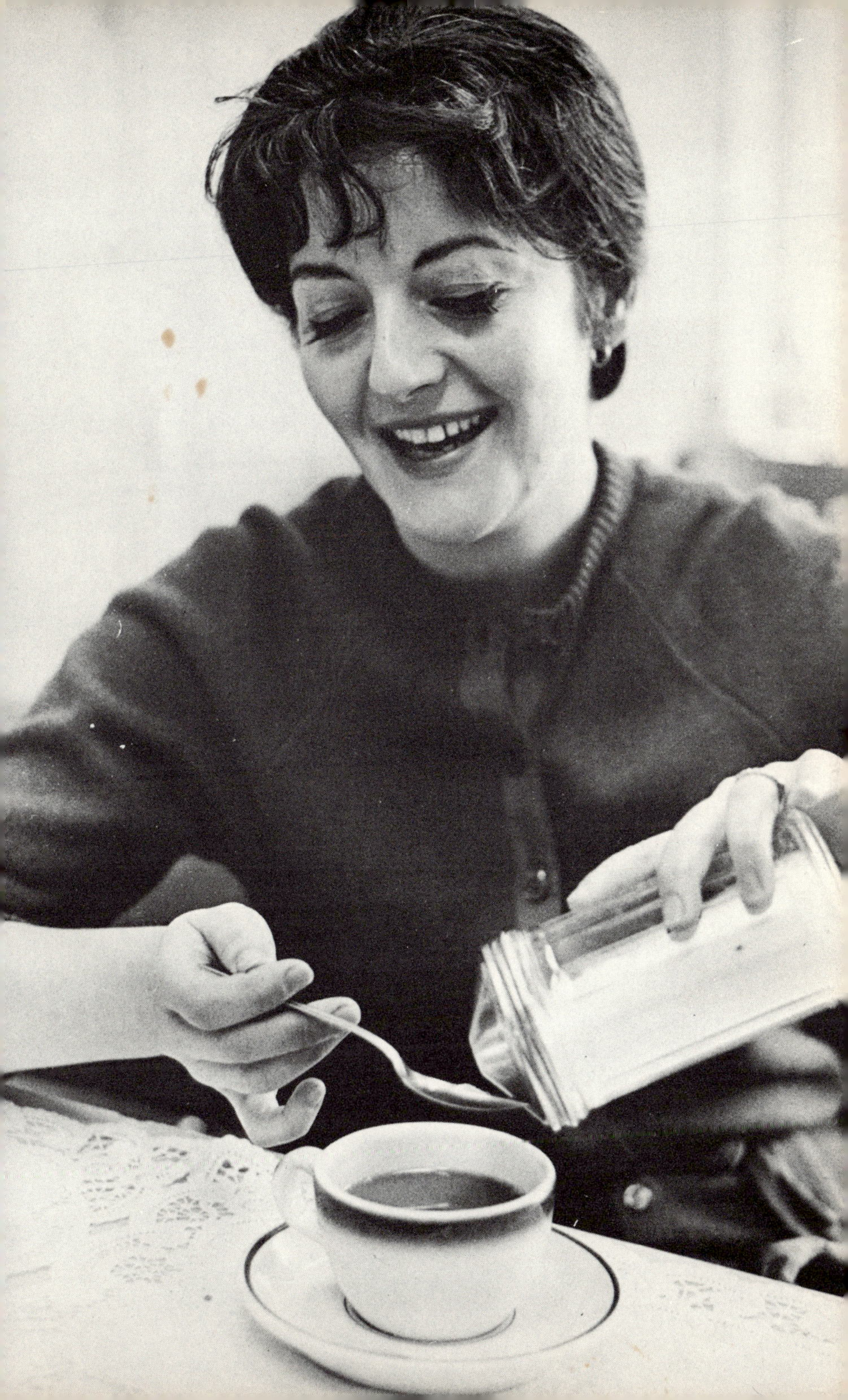

Everywhere there are indications
that feminism is an idea
whose time has come.
This is apparent not only
in the speed
with which the movement
has spread across the country
without any national
or centralized direction,
but also, and this is perhaps more interesting,
in the response of many
outside the movement.

                Karen Durgin

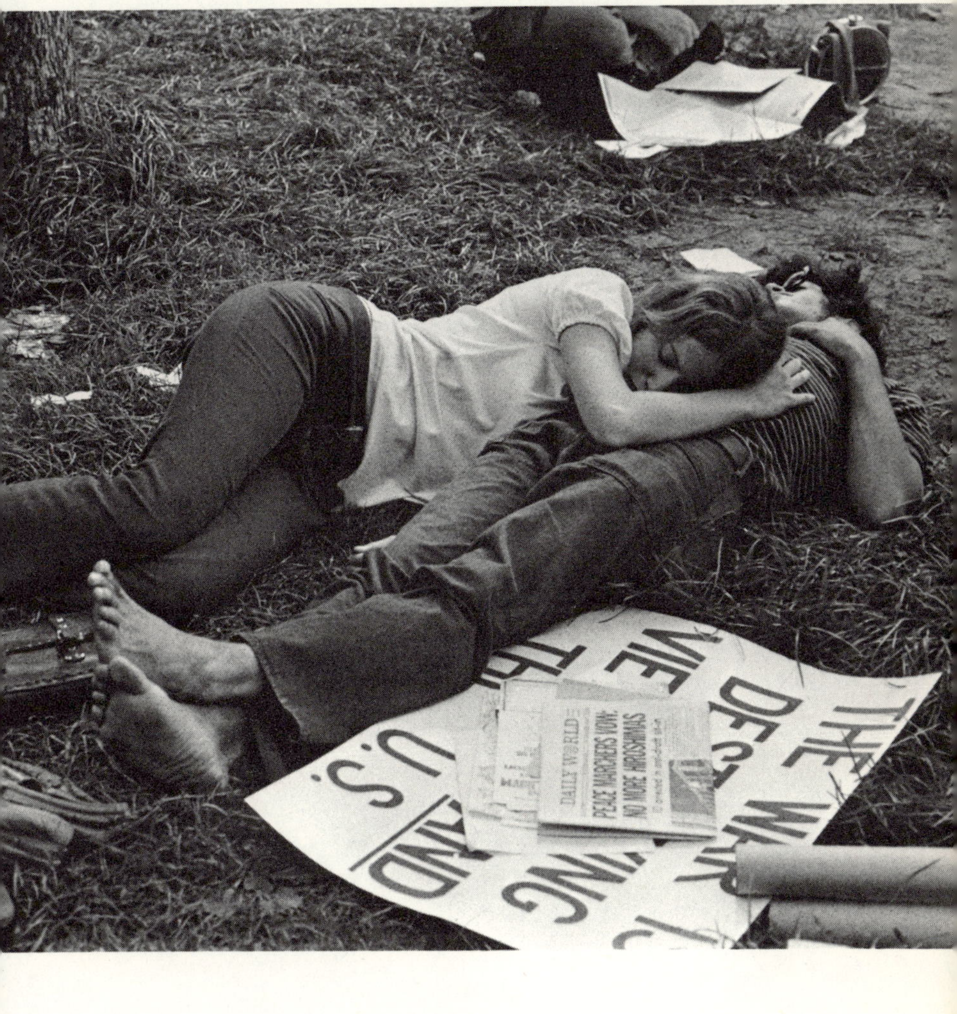
DAILY WORLD
PEACE MARCHERS VOW:
NO MORE HIROSHIMAS

5

RICH MAN, POOR MAN

Complaints From Various Quarters

All animals are equal
but some animals
are more equal than others.

George Orwell

And here it should be noted
that a prince ought never
to make common cause
with one more powerful than himself
to injure another,
unless necessity forces him to it . . .
for if he wins you rest in his power,
and princes must avoid
as much as possible being under
the will and pleasure of others.

Niccolo Machiavelli

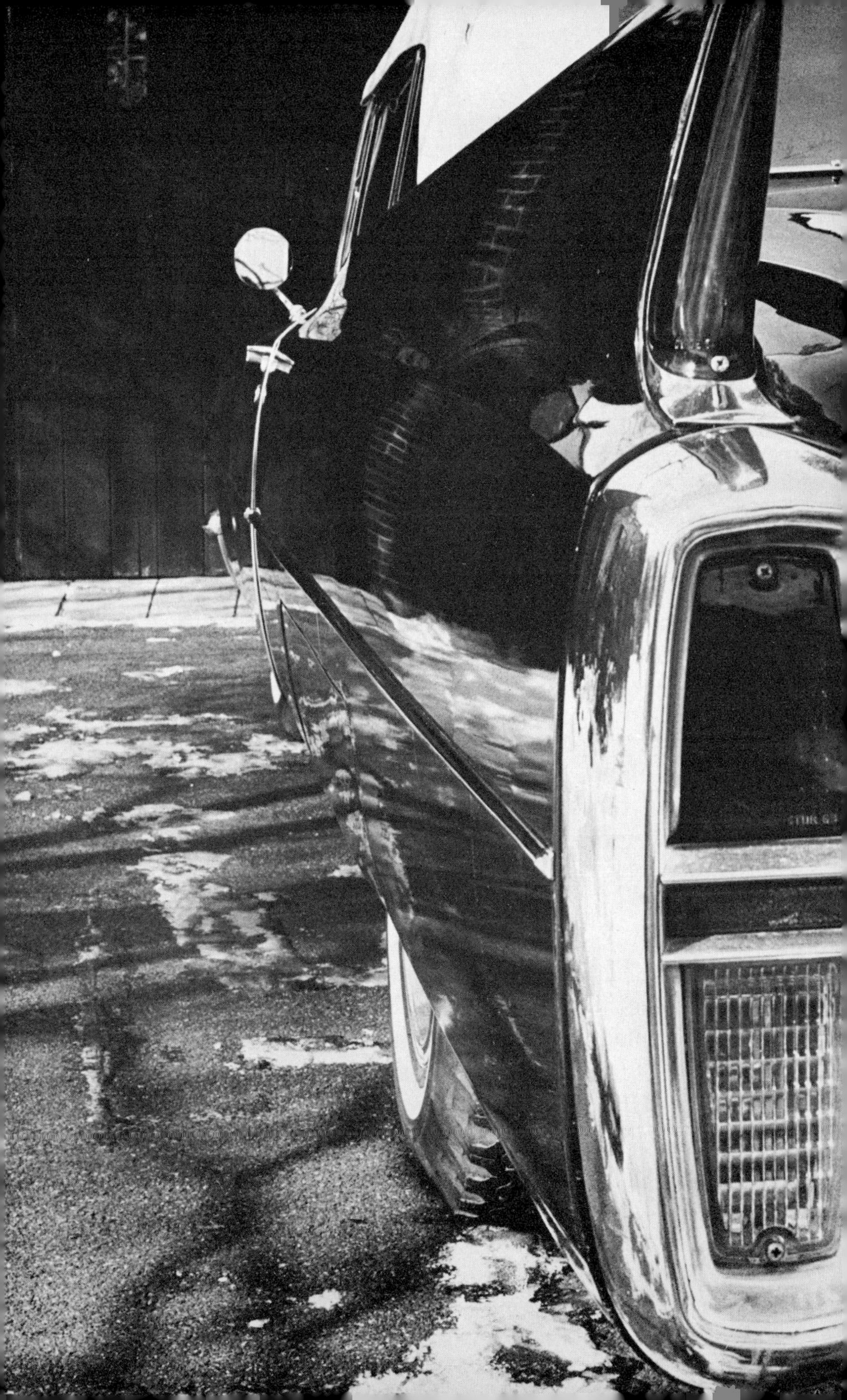

A series of *Look* research studies shows that the rulers of economic America—the producers, the financiers, the manufacturers, the bankers and the insurers—are still overwhelmingly WASP.

50 Largest Corporations. Of 790 directorships of these giants of business and industry, 88 per cent are held by apparent WASPs. The word "apparent" is used because definite ethnic lineage cannot be determined in some cases. Boards of 31 of the corporations are exclusively WASP. Nine others have one or more Jews on the board, while nine have one or more Catholics. The executives, like the directors, are mostly WASPs.

10 Largest Commercial Banks. Of 241 directorships, about 200, or 83 per cent, are held by WASPs. Of the remainder, Roman Catholics hold slightly more than Jews. An interesting case is that of the Bank of America, the nation's largest. It was founded by the late Amadeo Peter Giannini, son of Italian immigrants, under the name "Bank of Italy." By a combination of unorthodox retail methods and Italian flair, Giannini became the financial power of California. Today, the Bank of America is as heavily WASPish as its competitors.

5 Largest Life Insurance Companies. At least 100 of the 131 directorships are held by WASPs, and probably more. The WASP representation appears to be about 80 per cent.

Other studies in recent years have shown the economic dominance of the WASP to have become but slightly dented since the 1920's, when Mencken thought the Anglo-Saxon to be moribund. While minority entrepreneurs have moved strongly into such fields as entertainment, construction, retailing and research laboratories, the big money generated by basic production remains in WASP hands. One survey showed that less than one per cent of corporate executives in this country are Jewish, although Jews account for eight per cent of all college graduates, the chief source for executive talent. Studies by the American Jewish Committee show but a sprinkling of Jews in the executive suites of such specific businesses as the auto industry, public utilities, banking, insurance and shipping. While Catholic organizations do not undertake such surveys, the movement of the Irish and Italian minorities into corporate management appears to be only slightly more ample than that of the Jews. The Negro executive remains a rarity, as does the Mexican-American and the Puerto Rican.

Fletcher Knebel

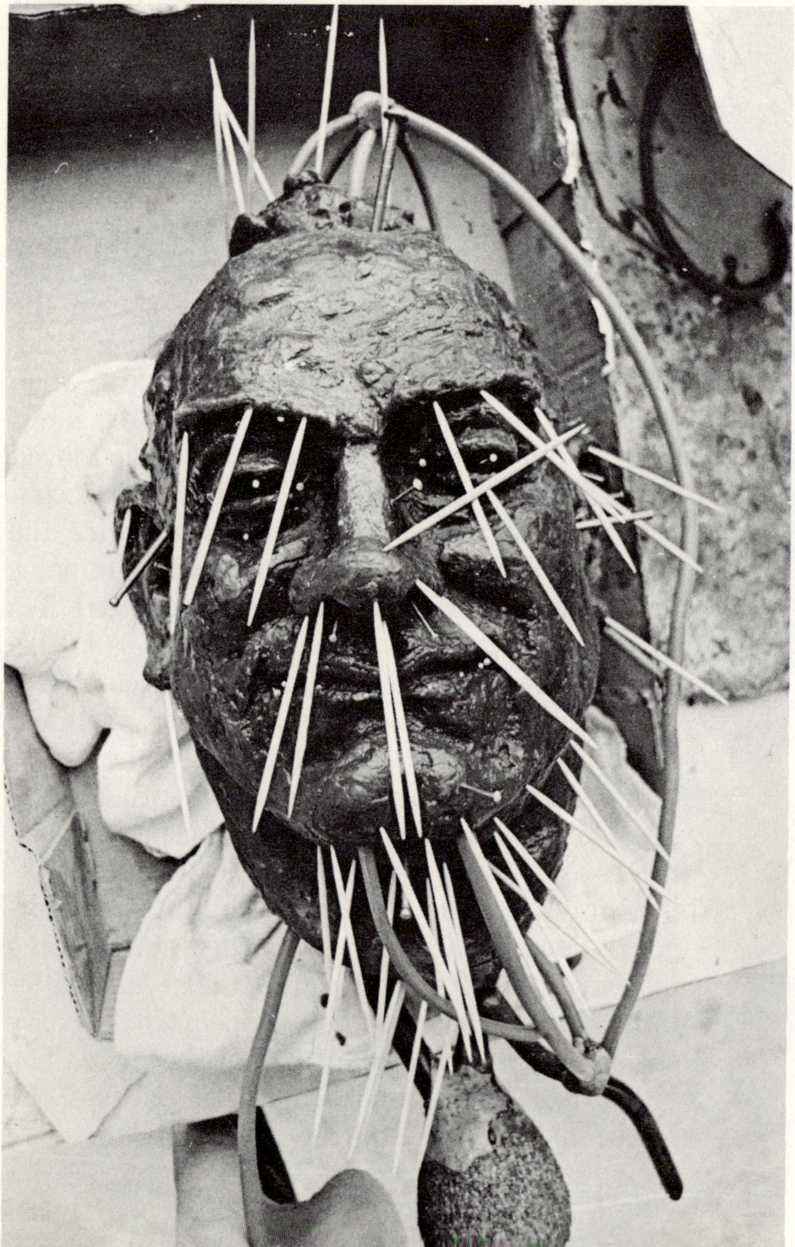

The motivation of art
as a commodity
is so strongly ingrained
that artists today accept
without blinking an eye
the financial support of corporations
and government agencies
involved in human destruction
and manipulations.
Yes, the artist is
as guilty of murder
as the businessman.

    John Hendricks

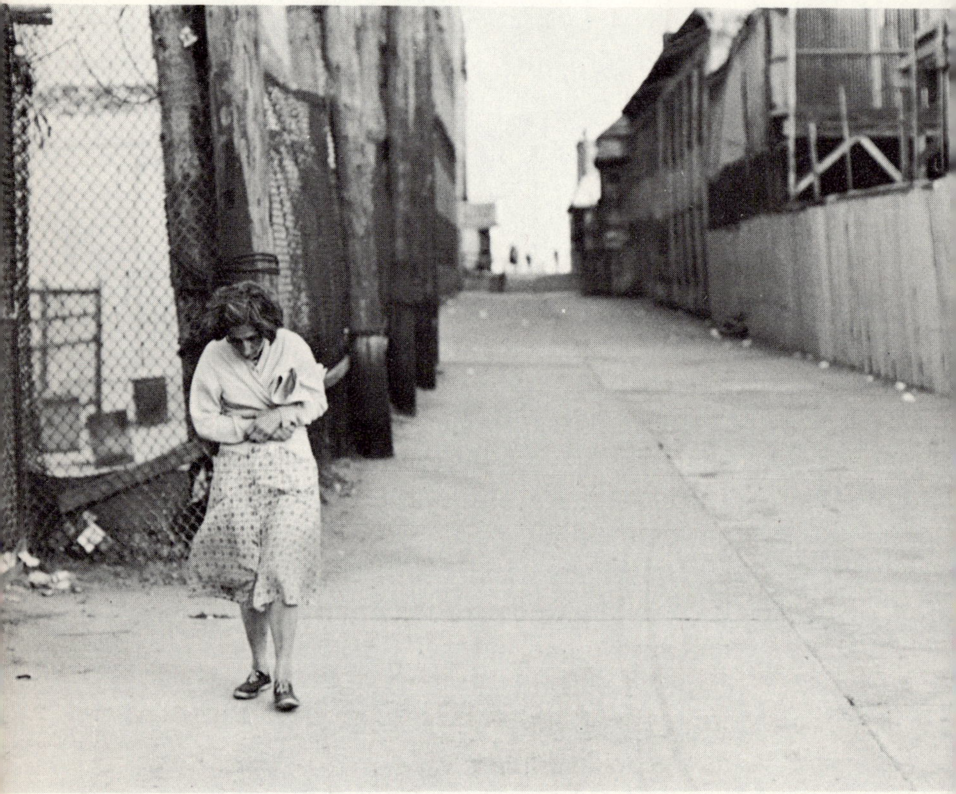

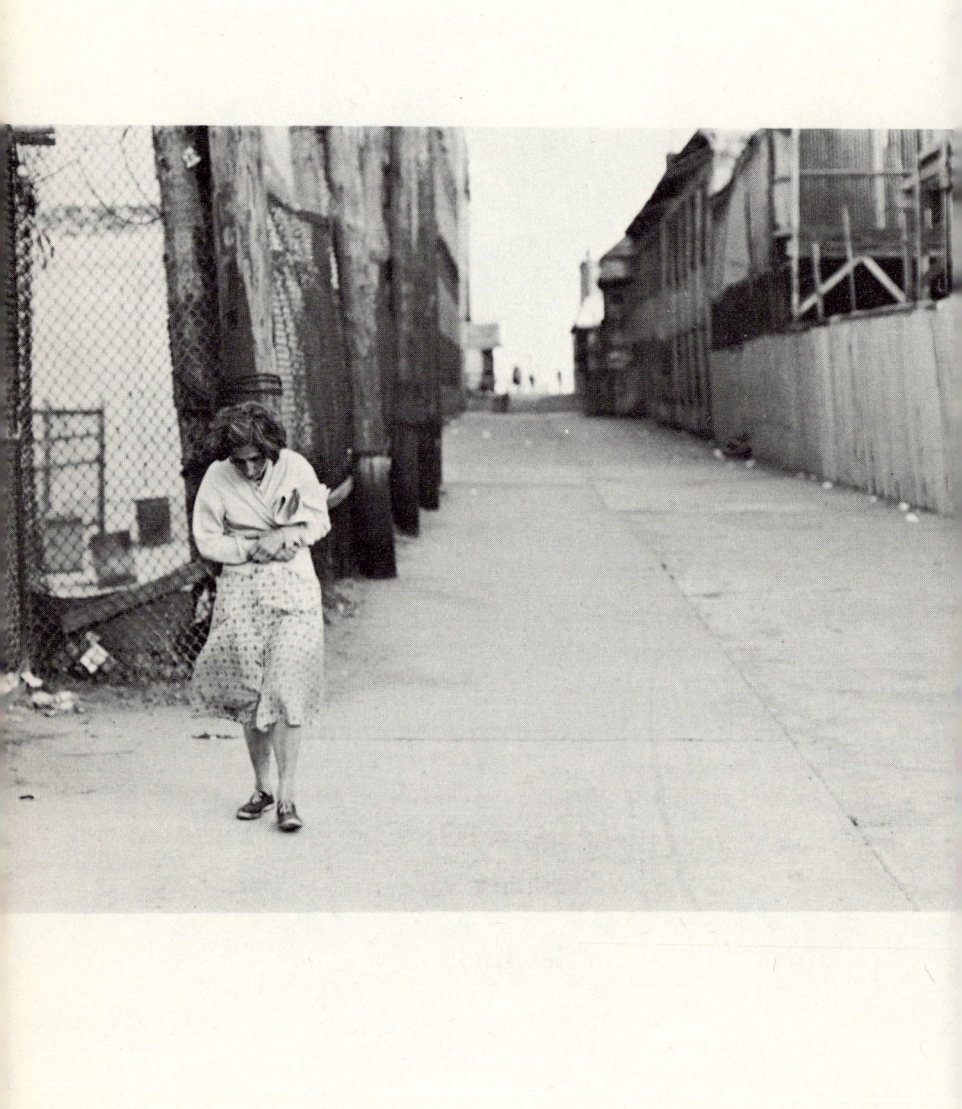

The working class and the employing class
have nothing in common.
There can be no peace
so long as hunger and want are found
among millions of working people
and the few, who make up the employing class,
have all the good things of life.
Between these two classes
a struggle must go on
until the workers of the world
organize as a class,
take possession of the earth
and the machinery of production,
and abolish the wage system.

        Industrial Workers of the World
        Preamble

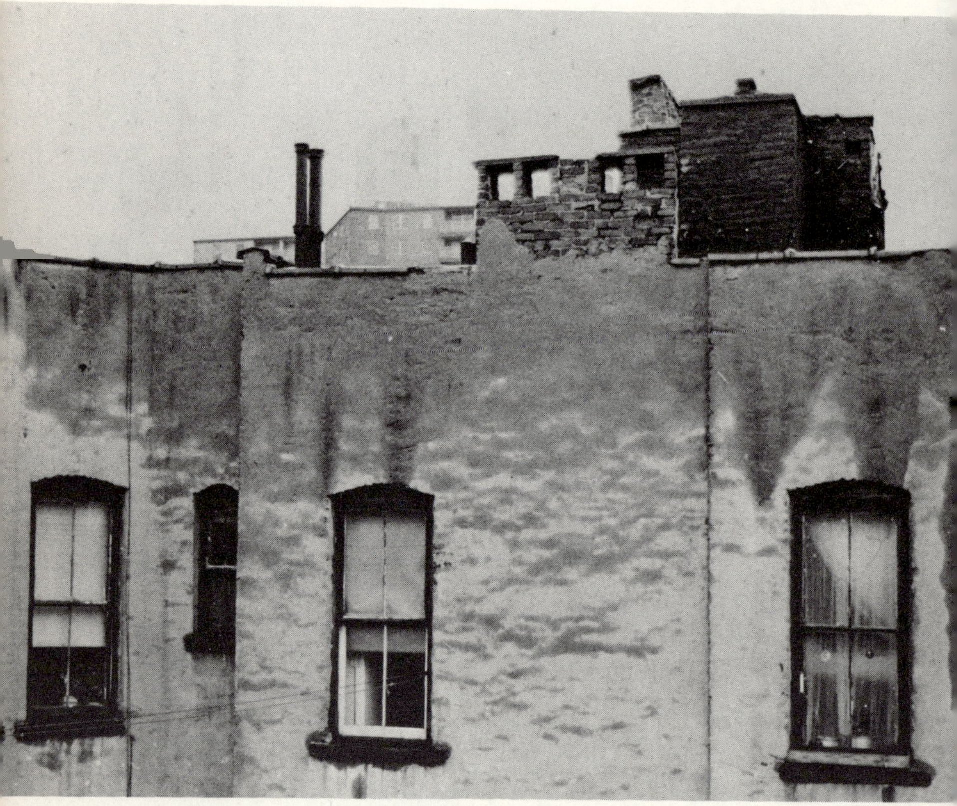

Home: Darkness and Light

O beautiful for spacious skies,
    for amber waves of grain,
For purple mountain majesties
    above the fruited plain!
America! America!
    God shed His grace on thee,
And crown thy good with brotherhood
    from sea to shining sea.

      "America the Beautiful"

    I like to see a man
    proud of the place
    in which he lives.
    I like to see a man
    who lives in it
    so that his place
    will be proud of him.

      Abraham Lincoln

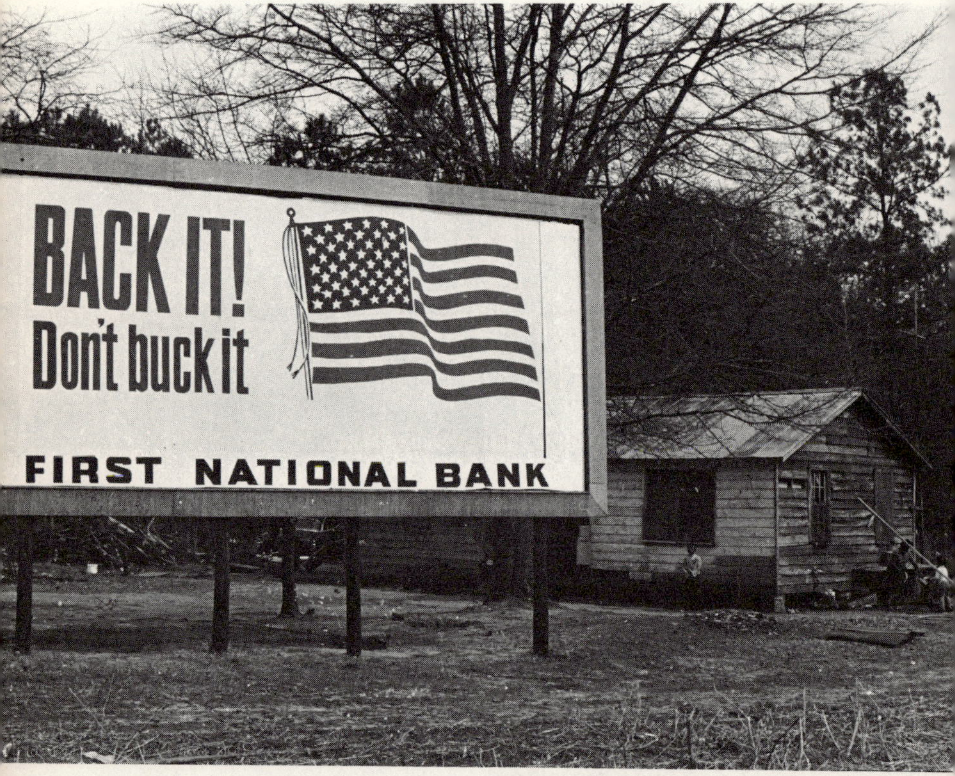
BACK IT!
Don't buck it
FIRST NATIONAL BANK

I know you, you cautious, conservative banks!
If people are worried about their rent it is your
    duty to deny them the loan of one nickel, yes,
    even one copper engraving of the martyred
    son of the late Nancy Hanks;
Yes, if they request fifty dollars to pay for a baby
    you must look at them like Tarzan looking at an
    uppity ape in the jungle,
And tell them what do they think a bank is, anyhow,
    they had better go get the money from their
    wife's aunt or uncle.
But suppose people come in and they have a million
    and they want another million to pile on top of it,
Why, you brim with the milk of human kindness and
    you urge them to accept every drop of it,
And you lend them the million so then they have two
    million and this gives them the idea that they
    would be better off with four,
So they already have two million as security so you have
    no hesitation in lending them two more,
And all the vice-presidents nod their heads in rhythm,
And the only question asked is do the borrowers
    want the money sent or do they want to take it withm.

                        Ogden Nash

So, the black man looks at television
and he sees those news reporters
saying the city is making a move
to inspect housing conditions,
and the man says that he thinks
everything is very deplorable
and he's going to make a move
to do something about it,
and he sets up a commission
or he appoints another inspector,
and then the days roll by
and the rat bites still show up on children,
and parents find
that they still have to sleep in shifts
to keep the rats away from the baby at night,
and the children are still catching pneumonia
in the winter because of the cold,
and are still not being able
to go to schools, which are inferior anyway ...
So where are the commissions,
and where are the inspectors
and where are the powers that be
that are supposed to effect the change?

                              Harlem girl, age 15

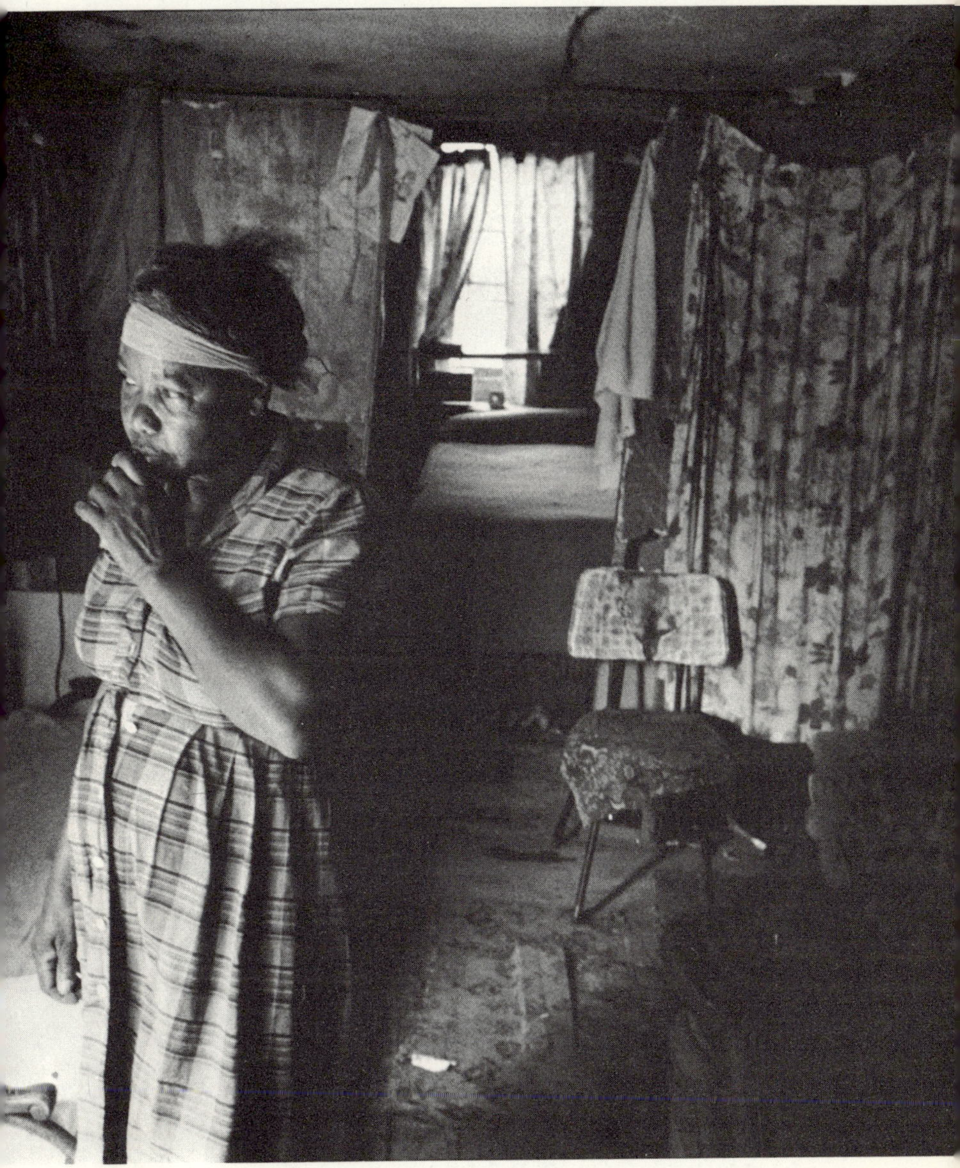

When you got nothing,
you got nothing to lose.
You're invisible now,
you got no secrets to conceal.

        Bob Dylan

When the sun breaks through
and streets are clean

When cities are bathed in light

When waters are no longer foul
and rivers carry no bodies

When the smoke is wafted away
and the stars shine in the sky

When trees are covered with leaves
parks and gardens burst with flowers
and fields are peopled with birds

When men in unison chant
the hymn of redemption

Then I will sing for you!

        João Accioli

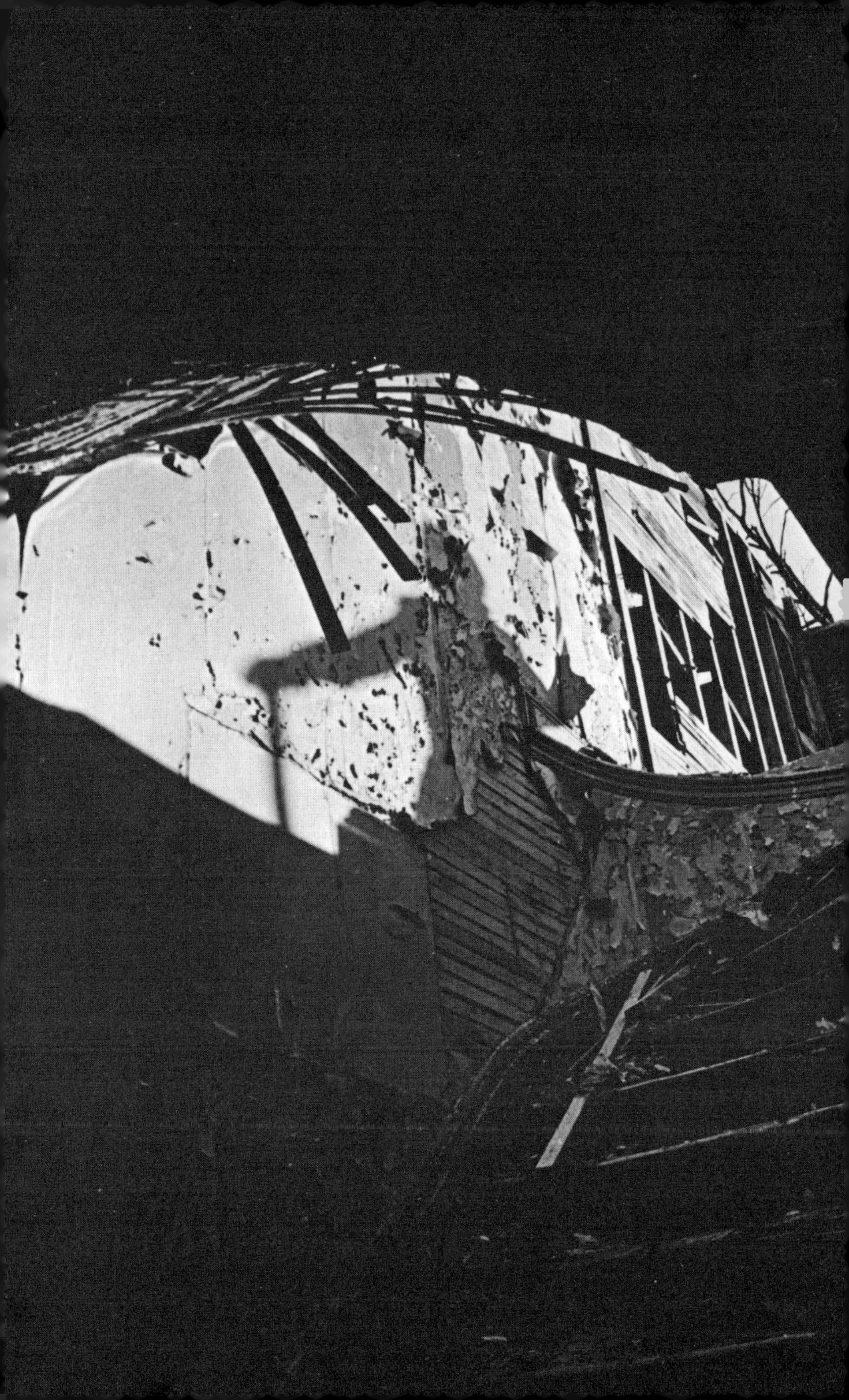

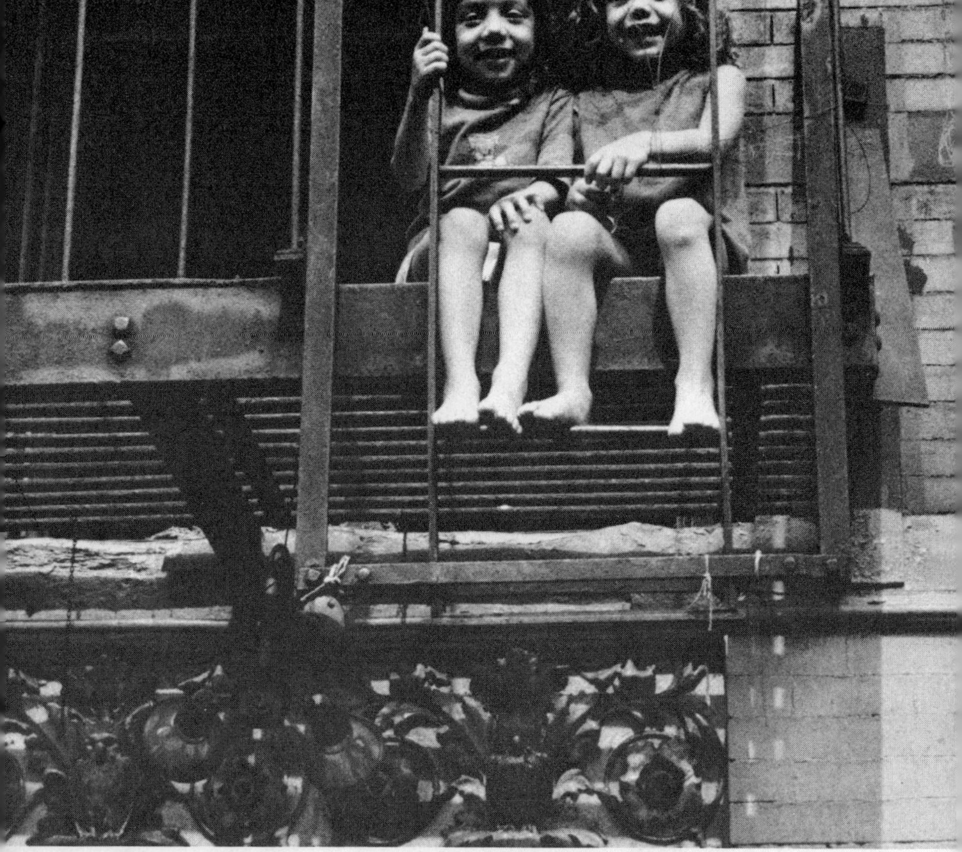

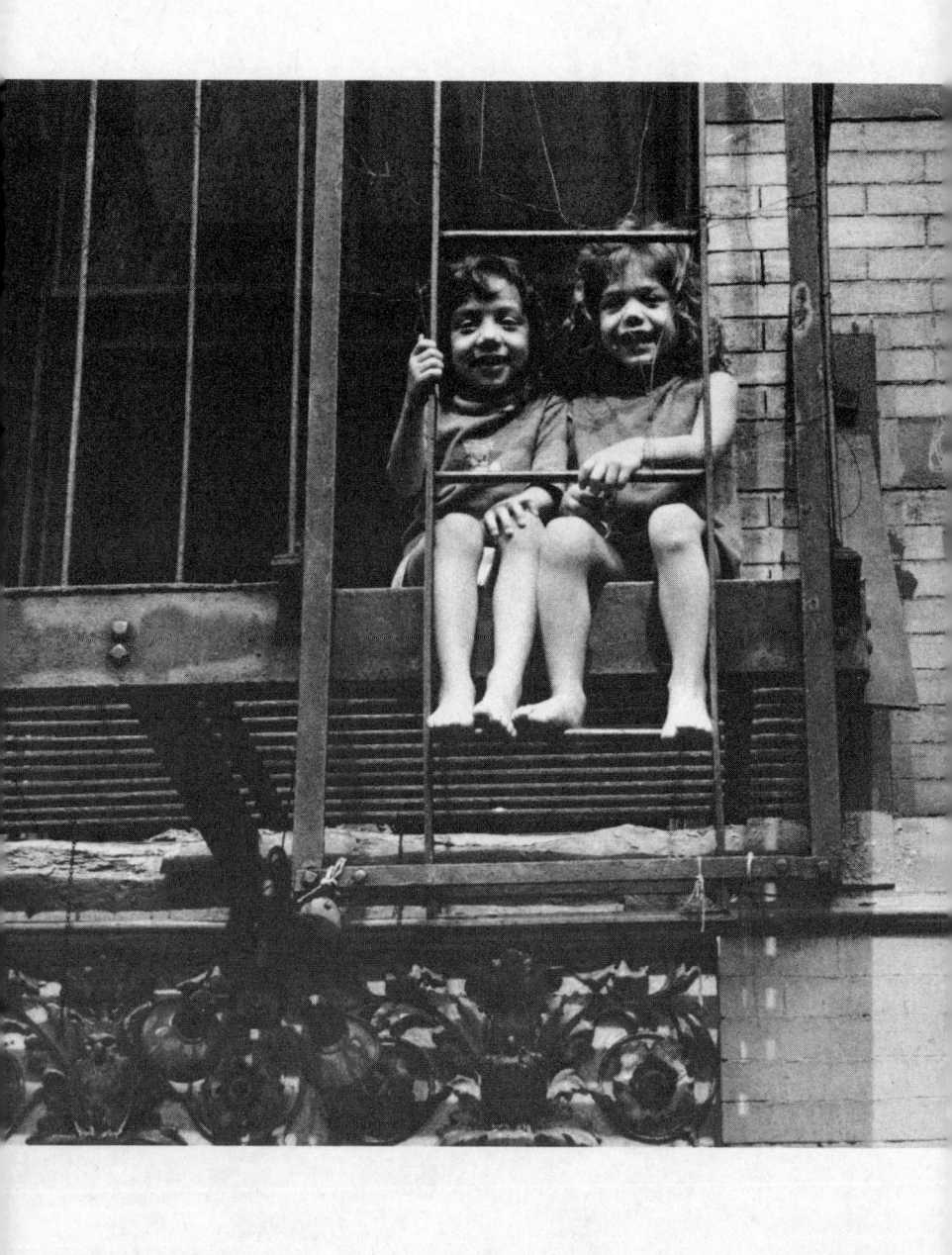

Beginning the Ascent

As the tree is fertilized
by its own broken branches
and fallen leaves,
and grows out of its own decay,
so men and nations
are bettered and improved
by trial,
and refined
out of broken hopes
and blighted expectations.

F. W. Robertson

Yet if the Great Ascent is slow,
cruel, even fearsome,
it is also irresistible,
stirring, grandiose.
It is an avenue of history
which, however difficult, leads
from an eternity of dark suffering
toward the possibility of light and life.
That it will surely usher in
a period of disorder, readjustment,
even temporary defeat
is as true for the fortunate few
as for the unfortunate many,
but it is also possible to see such a period
as prelude to a more distant era
in which, for the first time,
the potentialities of the entire human race
may be explored.
Thus if the trial is very great,
so is the ultimate prospect.

                        Robert L. Heilbroner

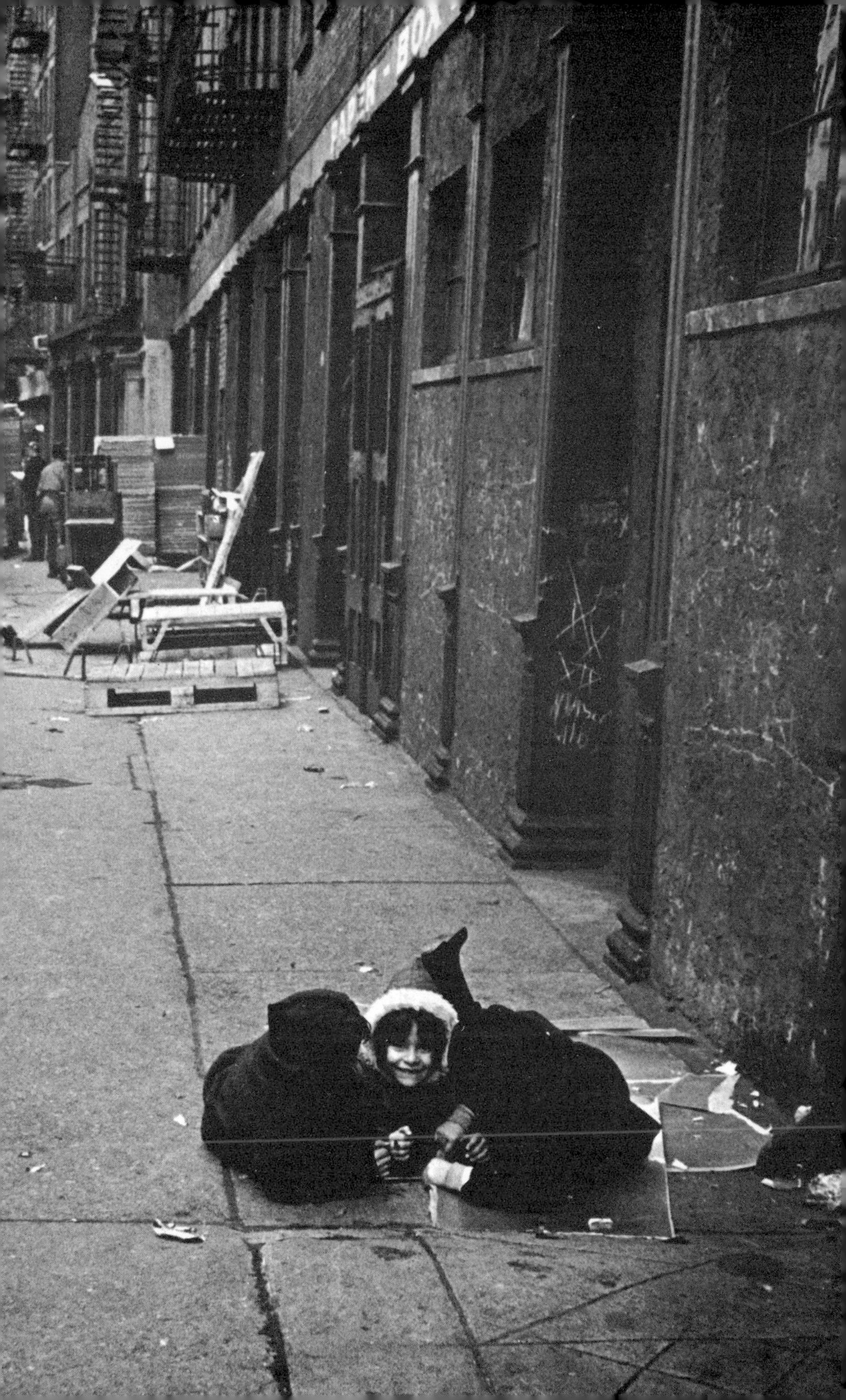

We could say that there are two principles
on which the whole social structure
must be based:
first, it is the human person
that is of supreme importance on earth
since the human person alone
has a divine destiny;
and every man and woman
has this destiny,
so that in this respect
all are equally important,
there are no class distinctions
in the kingdom of God.
Secondly, the human being
is made perfect through the love of God
and therefore through serving
the human family which is God's family;
so that, as one great man of prayer
expressed it, all our life should be work,
and all our work should be work for others.

                        Gerald Vann

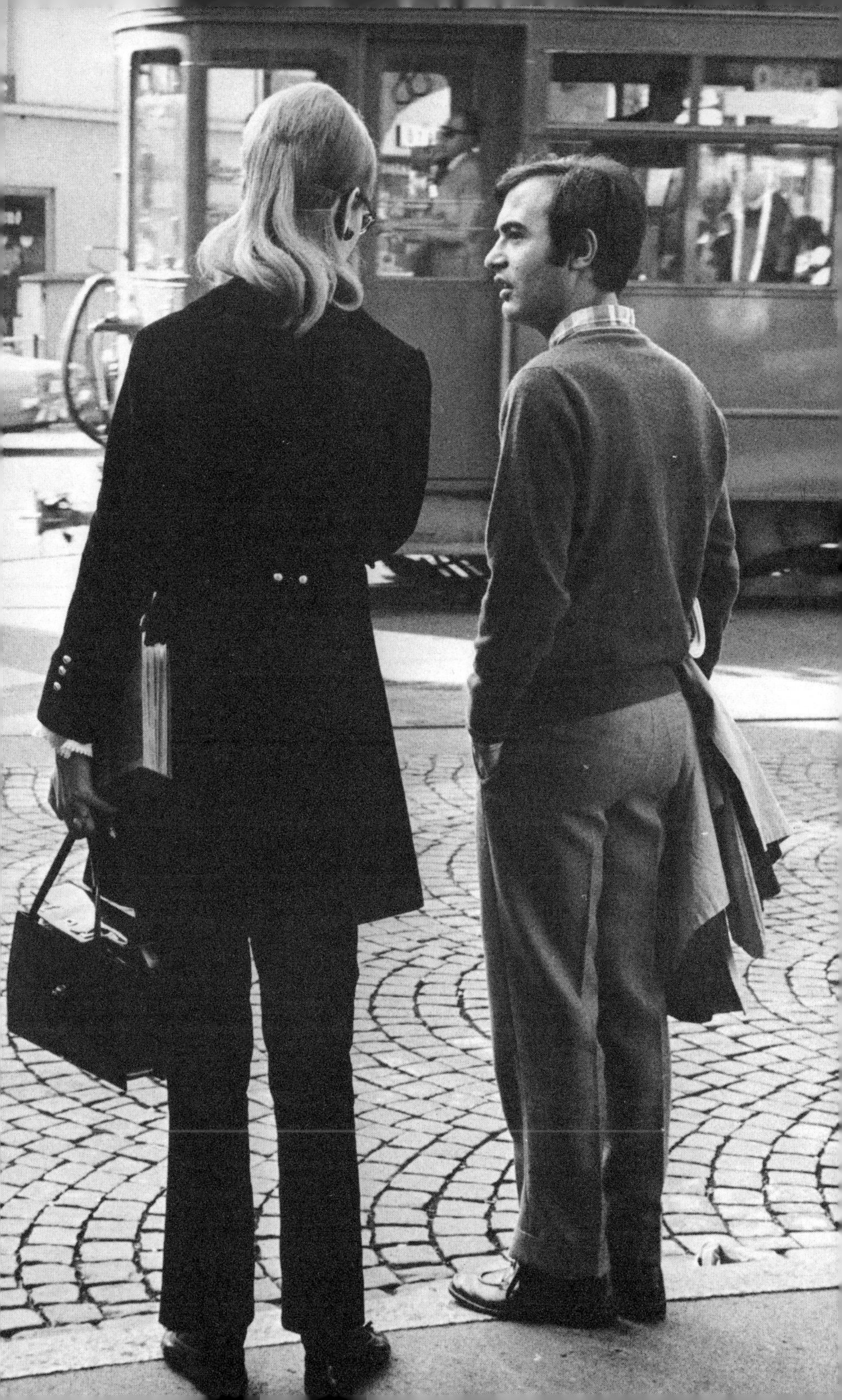

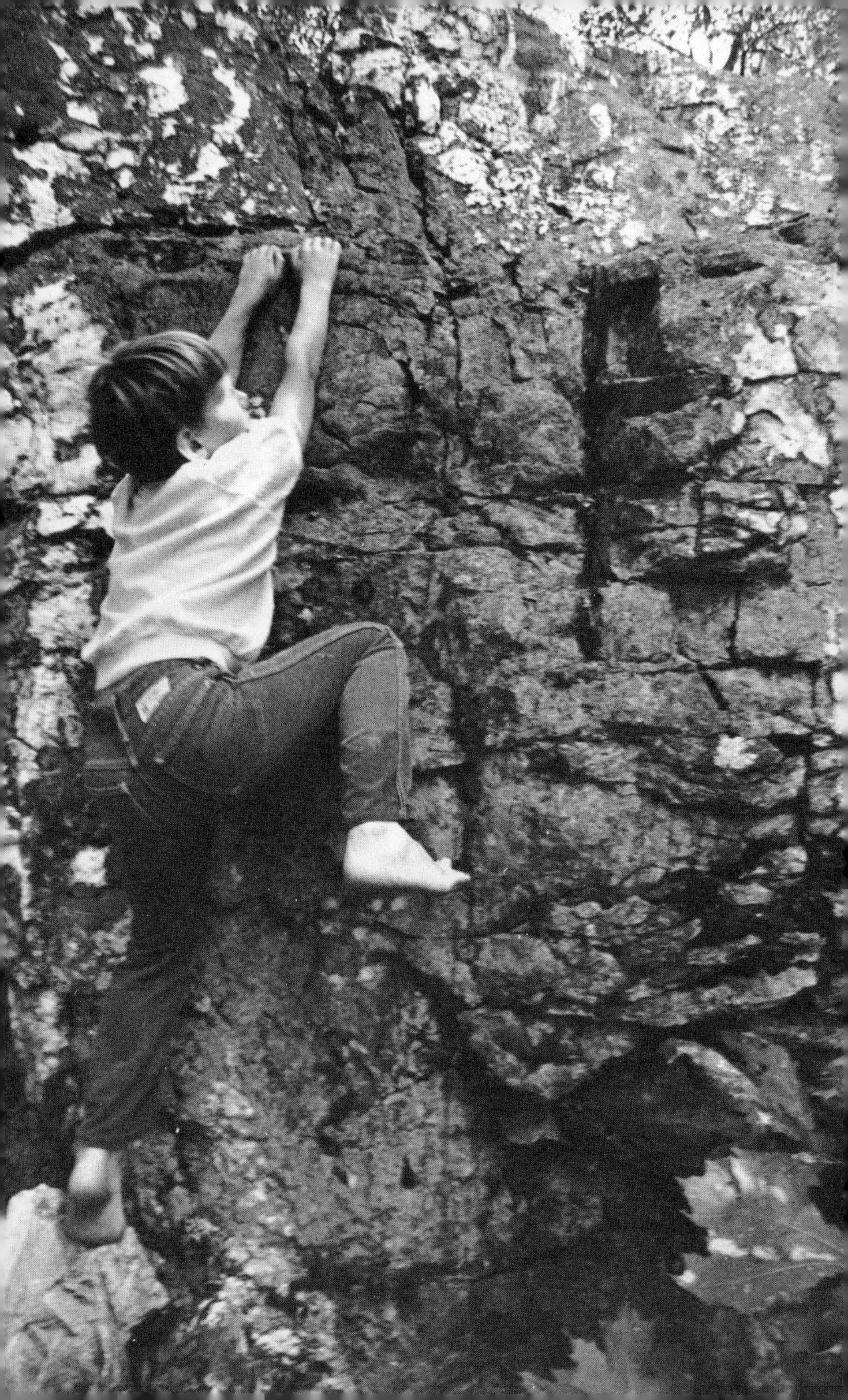

Key to evolution
adaptability:
the organism
alters itself
rather than continue
fruitless competition.

   Gary Snyder

There is new energy
being released in America
and the world;
it is bubbling up from the bottom.
It has begun to produce a chain reaction,
releasing still newer energies as it rises . . .
The most powerful,
the most inventive sources
are at the very bottom of the society . . .
What black brown yellow red poor white
     people are doing
is a source of hope;
we can imitate them.

               Kathy Mulherin

6

GENERATIONS APART

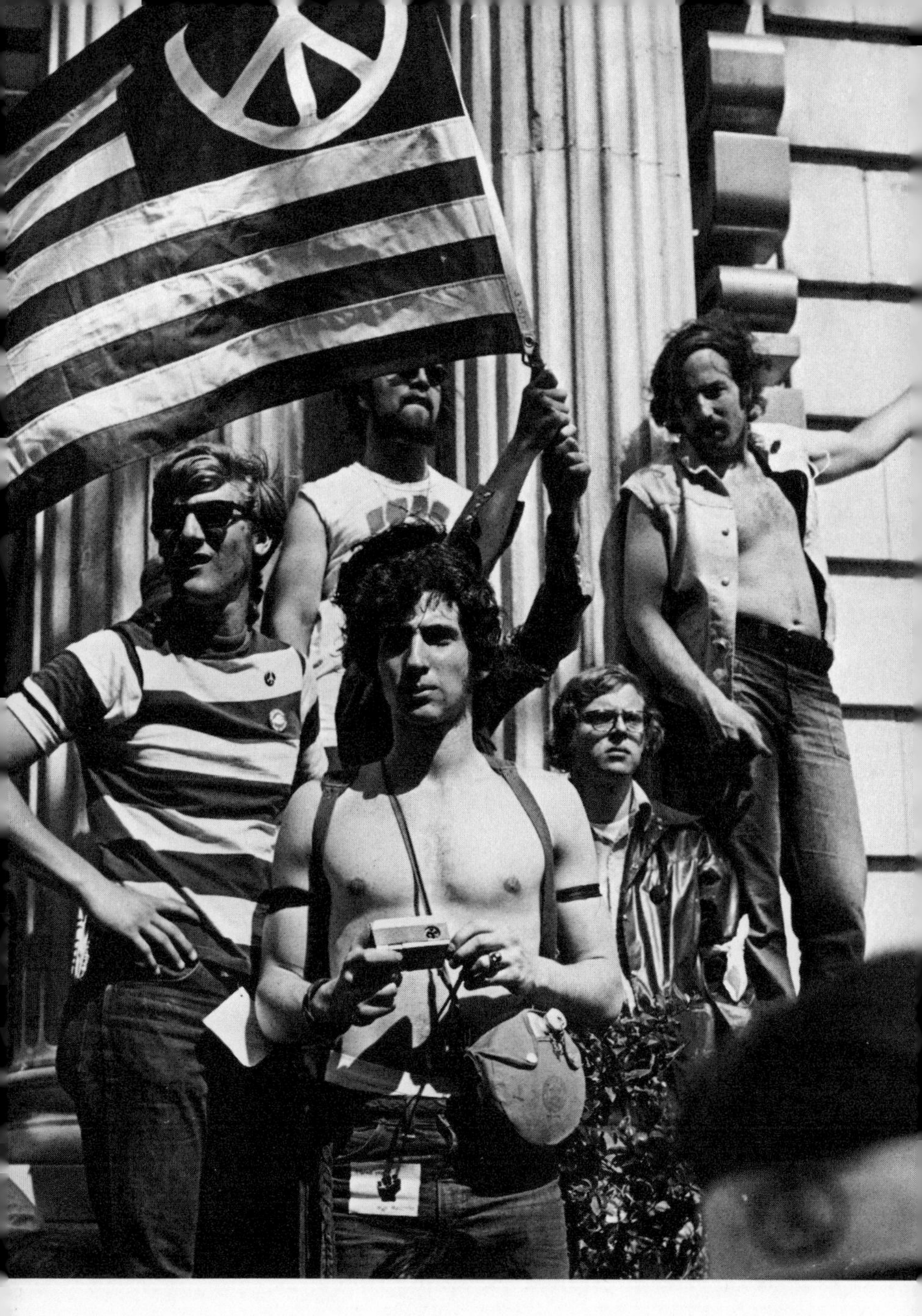

Parents and Other Strangers

The primary evidence
that our present situation is unique,
without any parallel in the past,
is that the generation gap is world-wide.
The particular events taking place in any country—
China, England, Pakistan, Japan,
the United States, New Guinea, or elsewhere—
are not enough to explain the unrest
that is stirring modern youth everywhere.

      Margaret Mead

  The city is infested
  by gangs of hardened wretches,
  born in the haunts of infamy.
  These fellows
   (generally youths
  between the ages
  of twelve and twenty-four)
  patrol the streets
  making night hideous.
  The police are intimidated
  by the frequency of these riots,
  the strength of the offenders.

        Philip Hone

I've heard a lot of crap
about listening to the young.
Hell, I've listened
till I'm sick of them.
They've got nothing to offer.

    Seabury H. Ford

There were a lot of points
that I tried to make in that song,
and a lot of them
didn't have to do with drugs.
A lot of them had to do with the relationship
between parents and their children.
Every one of the kids I spoke to then
had some kind of bad relationship
with their parents.
Some of them were just really sad,
and some of them I didn't use
because nobody would believe them
because they were so strong and so tragic.
The time you spend with your parents
really molds you,
that's when you're the softest and most pliable,
and all these kids had sores.

               Neil Diamond

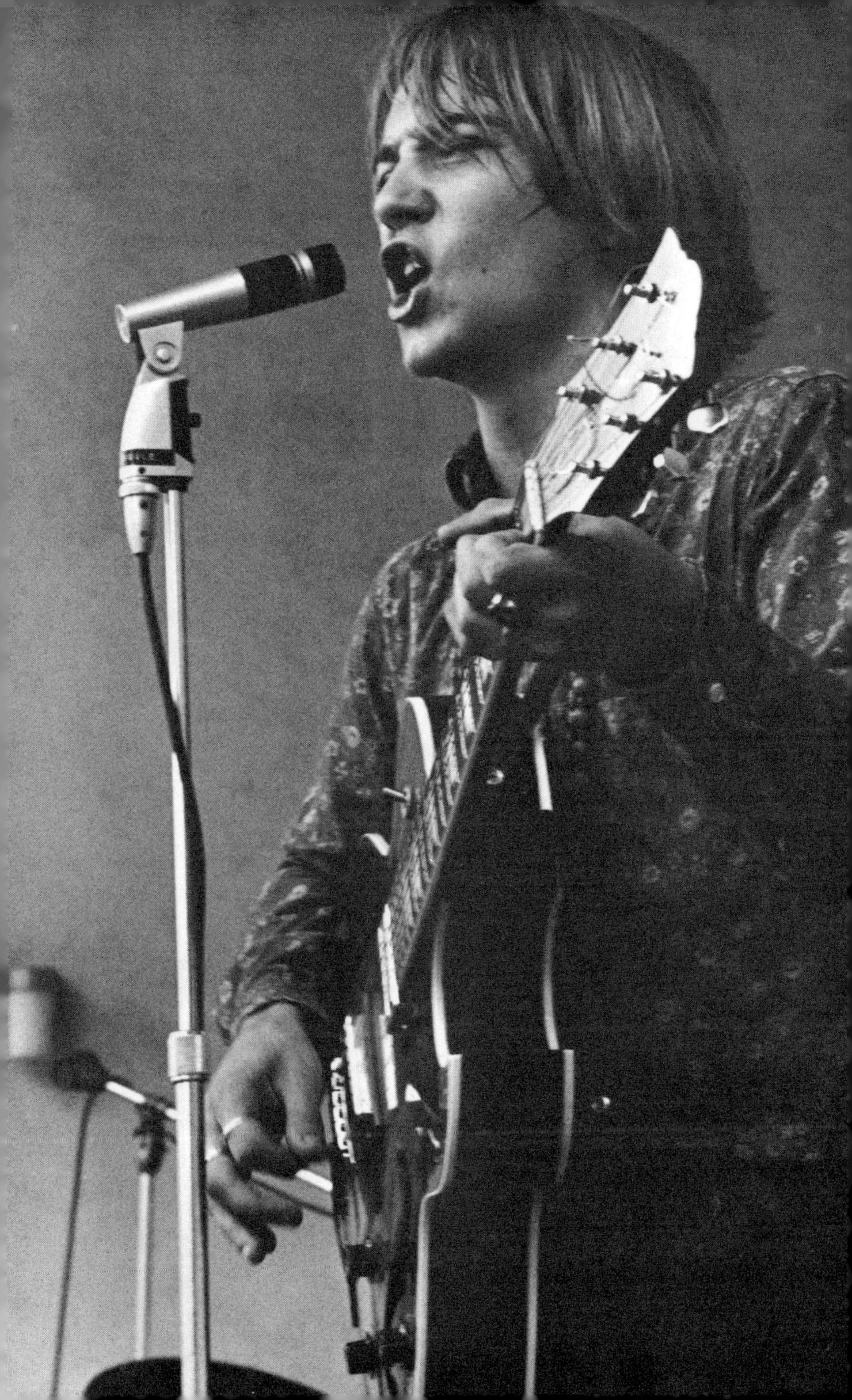

Mama seemed silly to me.
She was bothered
because most of the parents in the neighborhood
didn't allow their children to play with me.
What she didn't know was
that I never wanted to play with them.
My friends were all daring like me,
tough like me, dirty like me, ragged like me,
and had a great love for trouble like me . . .
We didn't think of ourselves as kids.
The other kids my age
were thought of as kids by me.
I felt that since I knew
more about life than they did,
I had the right to regard them as kids.

        Claude Brown

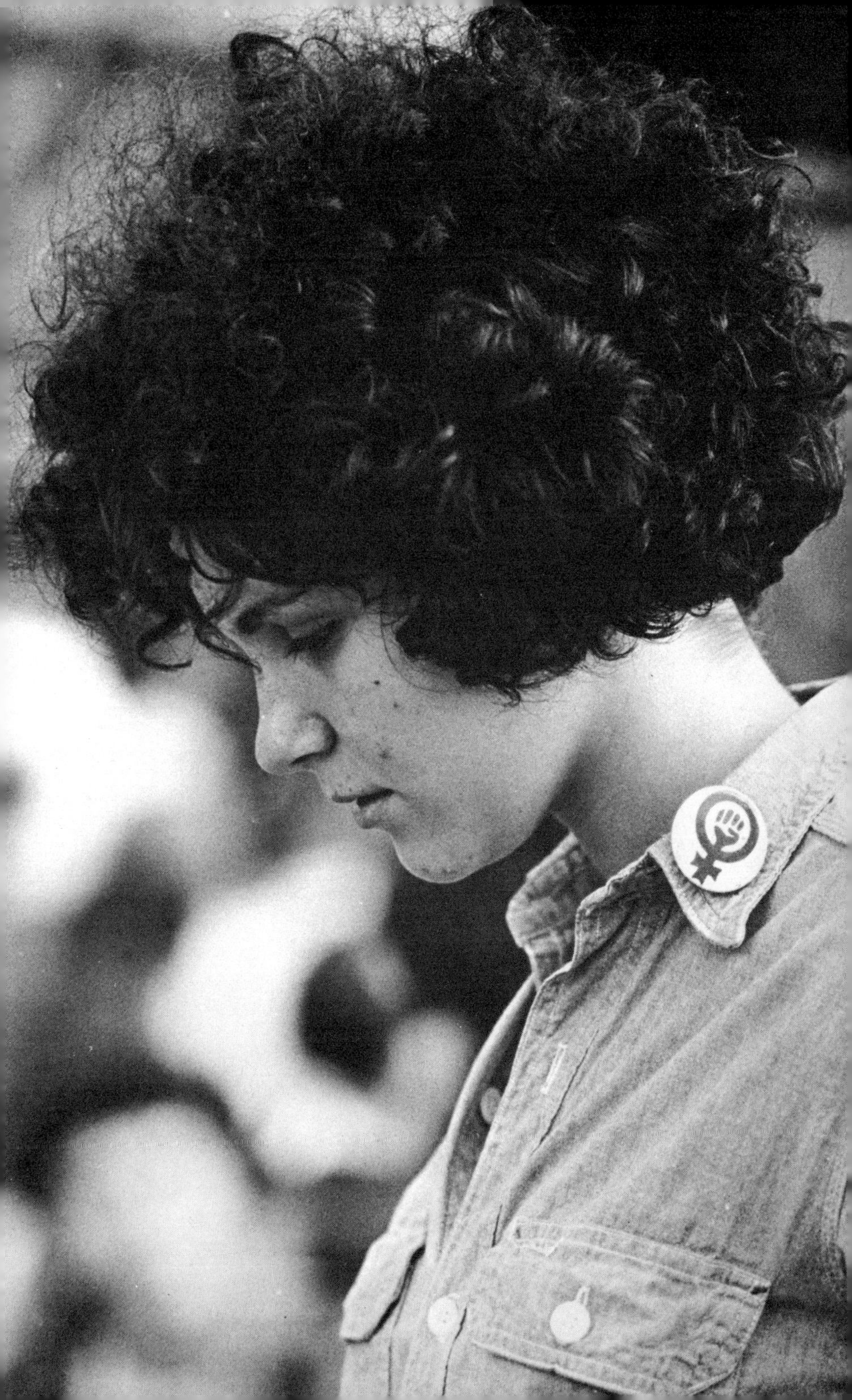

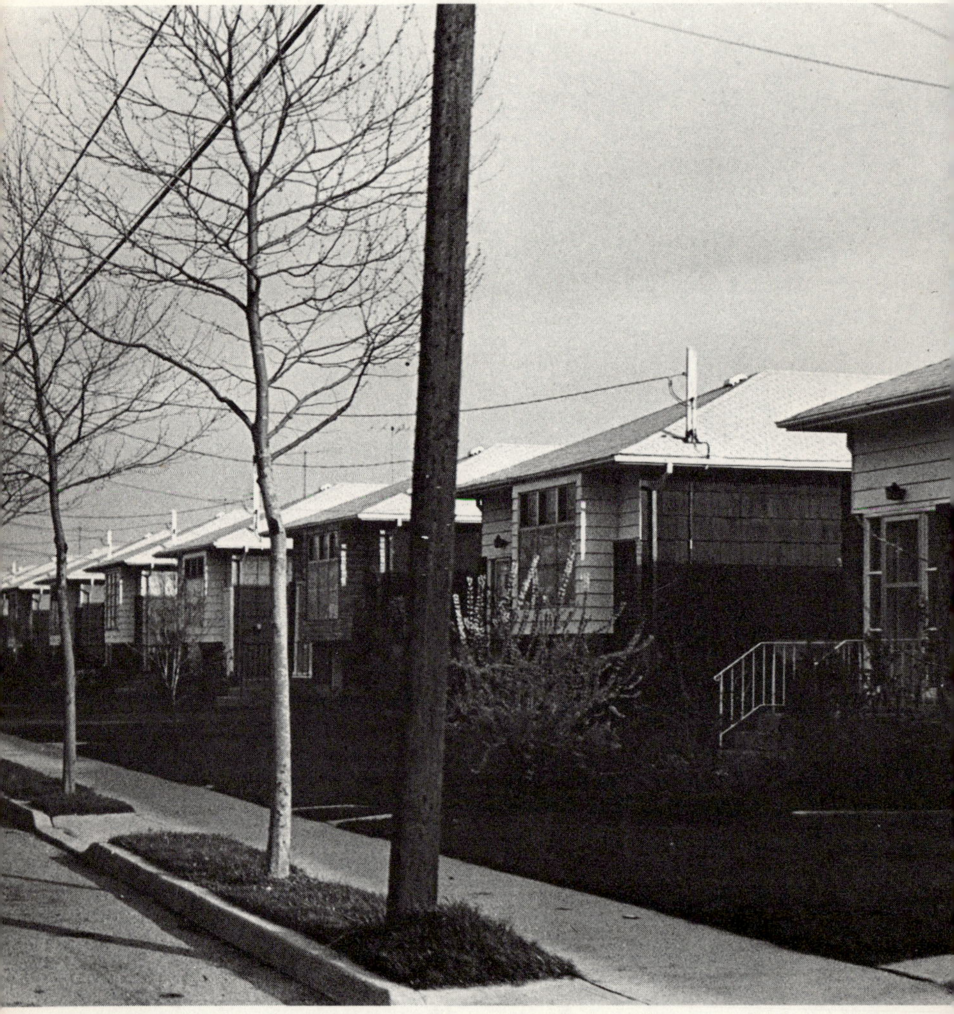

Kids and parents no longer communicate.
Young people run away from home
or stick it out silent, hostile,
involved in a world totally alien
to that of their parents;
a world that parents
are able to enter
only on their children's terms
(as some do, to the happiness of all).

                Martin Jezer

Then there was the suburban parent
running around in the movie
"Lovers and Other Strangers"
and compromising his manhood
and collaring the kids,
pretending to be thinking young
on everything, and saying,
"No gap! No gap!"

                Tony Miller

The longer I live
the more keenly I feel
that whatever was good enough
for our fathers
is not good enough for us.

                    Oscar Wilde

The young leadership is not satisfied.
I don't understand what they really want,
what it would take to satisfy them.

                              Jewel Drake

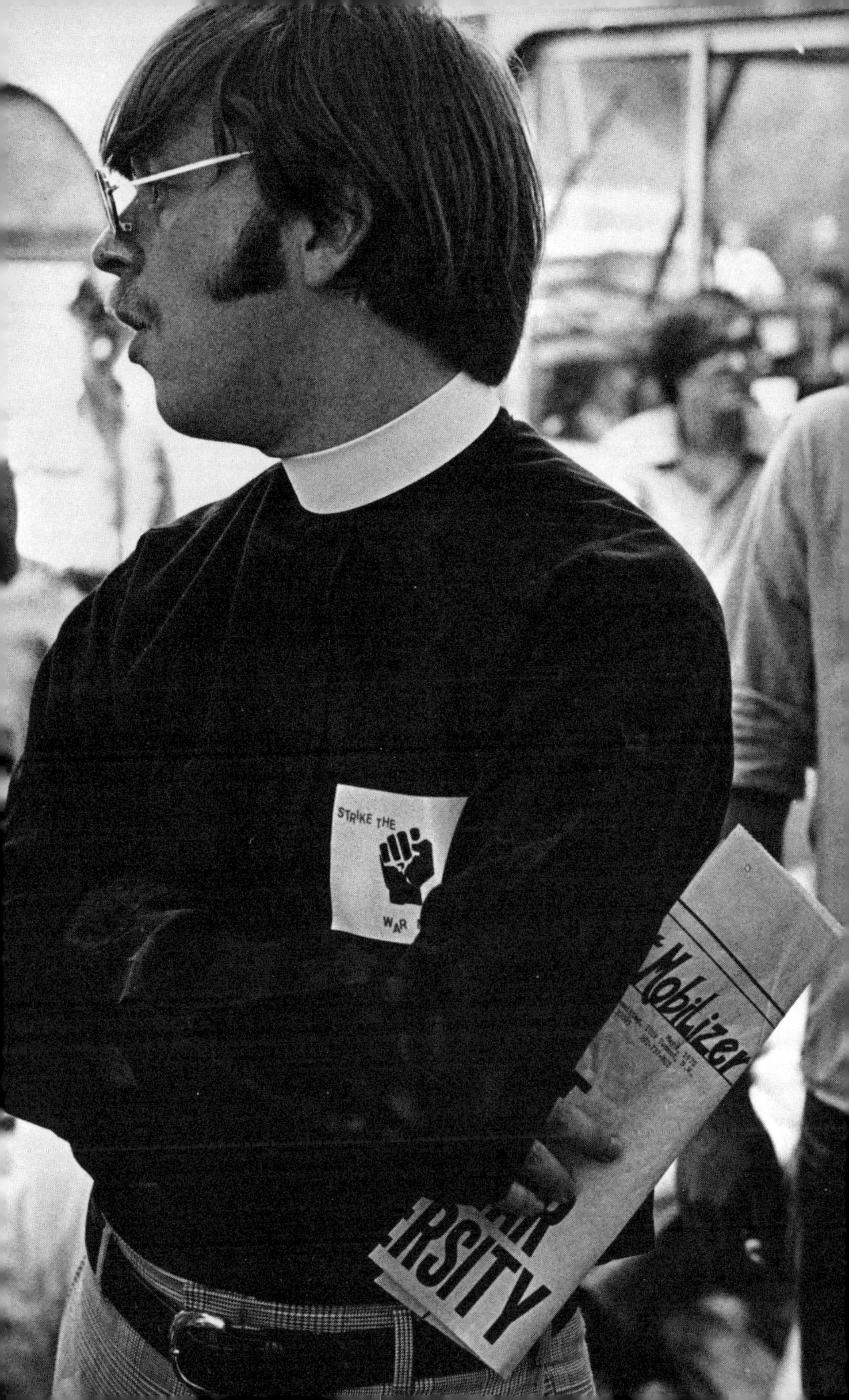
STRIKE THE
WAR
Mobilizer
RSITY

UAW SUPPORTS
FULL EMPLOYMENT
AND
GUARANTEED
ANNUAL
INCOME
EVERY AMERICAN

What We Are Doing

What we are doing
is creating new institutions,
new ways for people
to deal with one another...
We don't believe in private property.

                Jerry Weisgraw

What rock was doing
was concretizing our feeling
that the limits
were nowhere near being probed,
much less passed through:
it redefined for us the uptightness
of the straight world
and poured out in stark dimension
what they were all about:
if they got upset
about our hair and music,
what would they do to us
once we began telling them
how ridiculous
we thought it all was
in this society,
how narrow were their limits,
their vision,
their concept of freedom.

                Jonathan Eisen

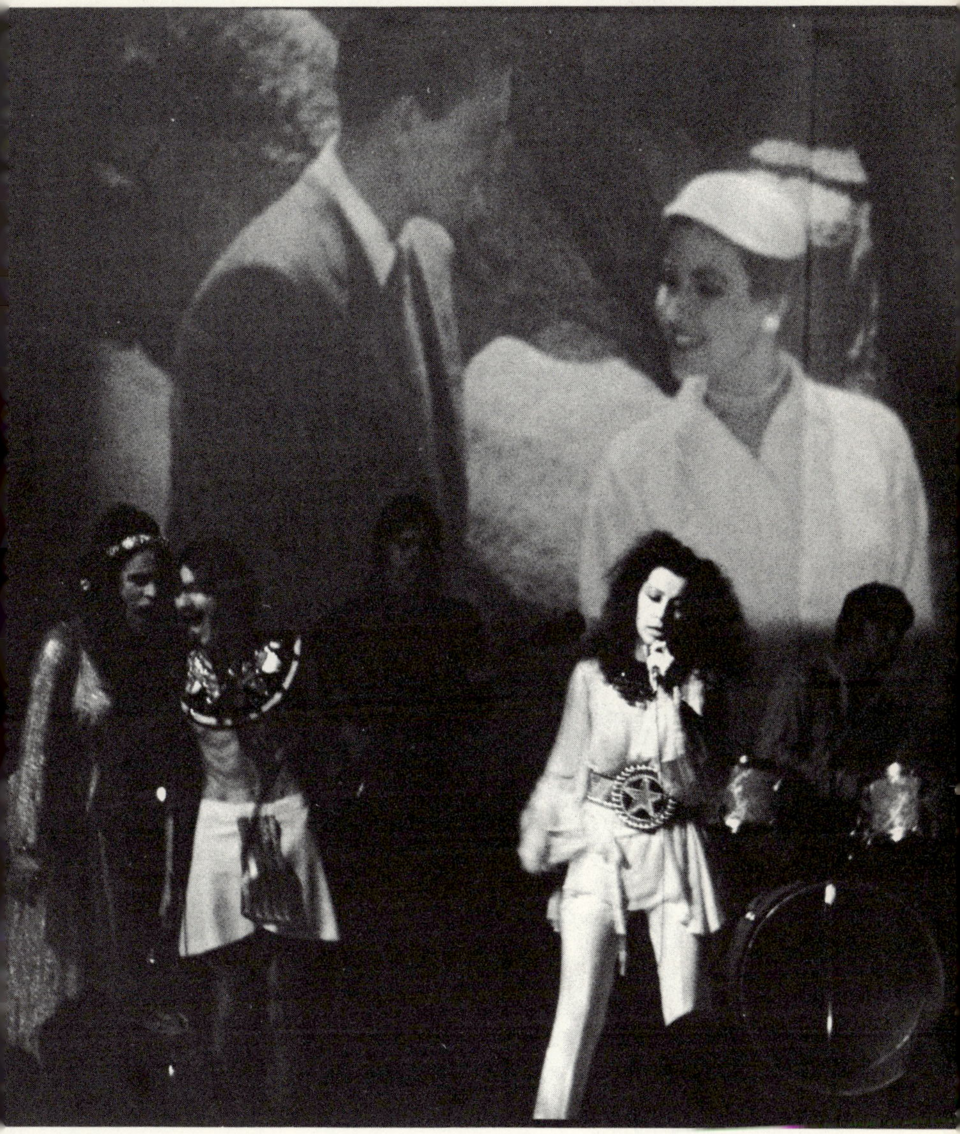

Rock represents freedom—
the freedom to feel,
to be one,
with a higher, collective force,
to move together in one cosmic rhythm.
It bridges ideologies
and personal differences.
It is the unifying love force
that gives us,
through the living experience,
the sensation of being oneself
and more than oneself
at the same time.

      Alan Oken

When Ringo sang,
"I get by with a little help from my friends,"
everybody flashed on the implications.
We were something new in the world,
adrift from the established society.
We had our friends,
or we had nothing.
And our friends became our family
and our families became a tribe,
and when a half million of us
surfaced at Woodstock...
we realized we had become a Nation.
Woodstock Nation, Abbie Hoffman calls us.

        Martin Jezer

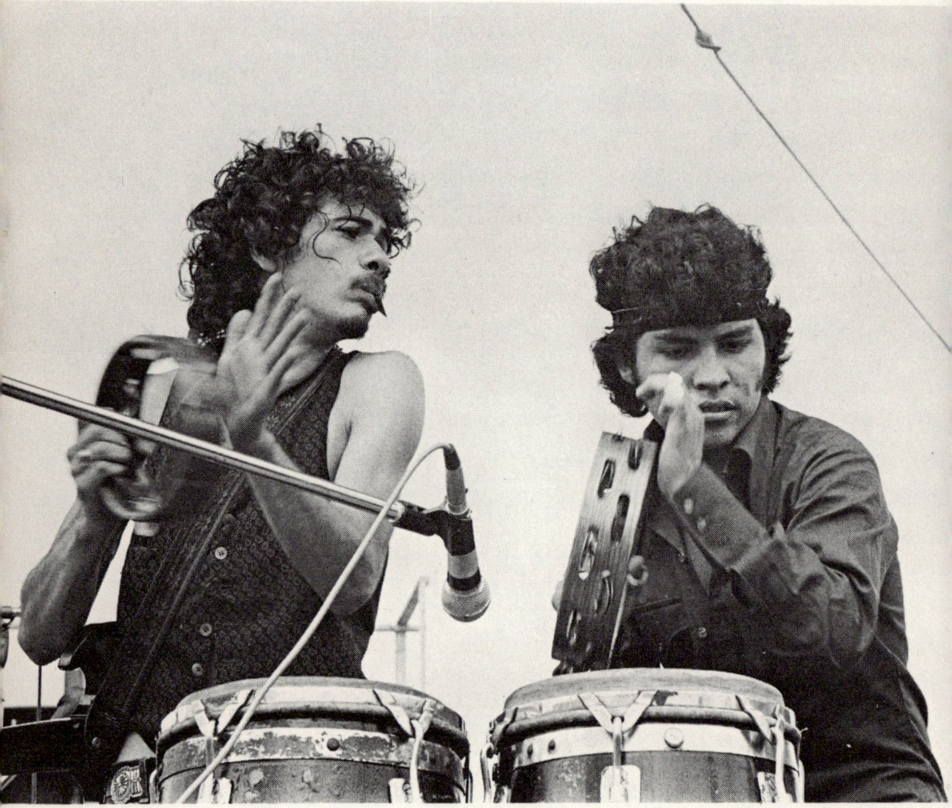

As a group we have never tried to preach.
Neither do we give out profundities.
At best what Steppenwolf do
is to give complete moral support
to the existing attitudes and philosophies
of today's misunderstood American youth...
At the moment I'm only aware of
Jefferson Airplane, Country Joe and ourselves,
who have anything positive to say
in terms of taking a political stand.

                                John Kay

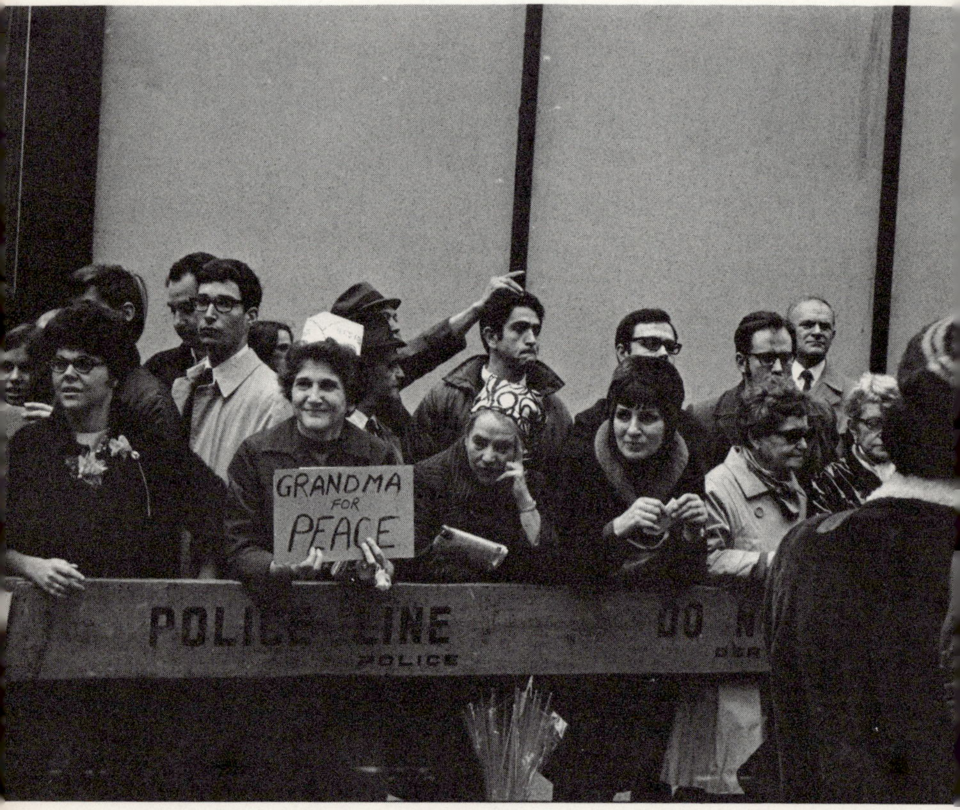
GRANDMA
FOR
PEACE
POLICE

Points of Convergence

My children awakened me three years ago
to the realization of how great the concern is,
how deep the love of country
and the desire to protect it.

        Thomas P. O'Neill

Finally my son got through to me.
I realized that I didn't understand this war
or believe that it was serving
the nation's vital interests.

        Edward H. Harte

Only the most radical
historical knowledge
can make us aware
of our extraordinary tasks
and preserve us
from a new wave
of mere restoration
and uncreative imitation.

        Martin Heidegger

The secret of a good life
is to have the right loyalties
and to hold them
in the right scale of values.
The value of dissent and dissenters
is to make us reappraise those values
with supreme concern for the truth . . .
But rebellion per se is not a virtue.
If it were, we would have
some heroes on very low levels.

        Norman Thomas

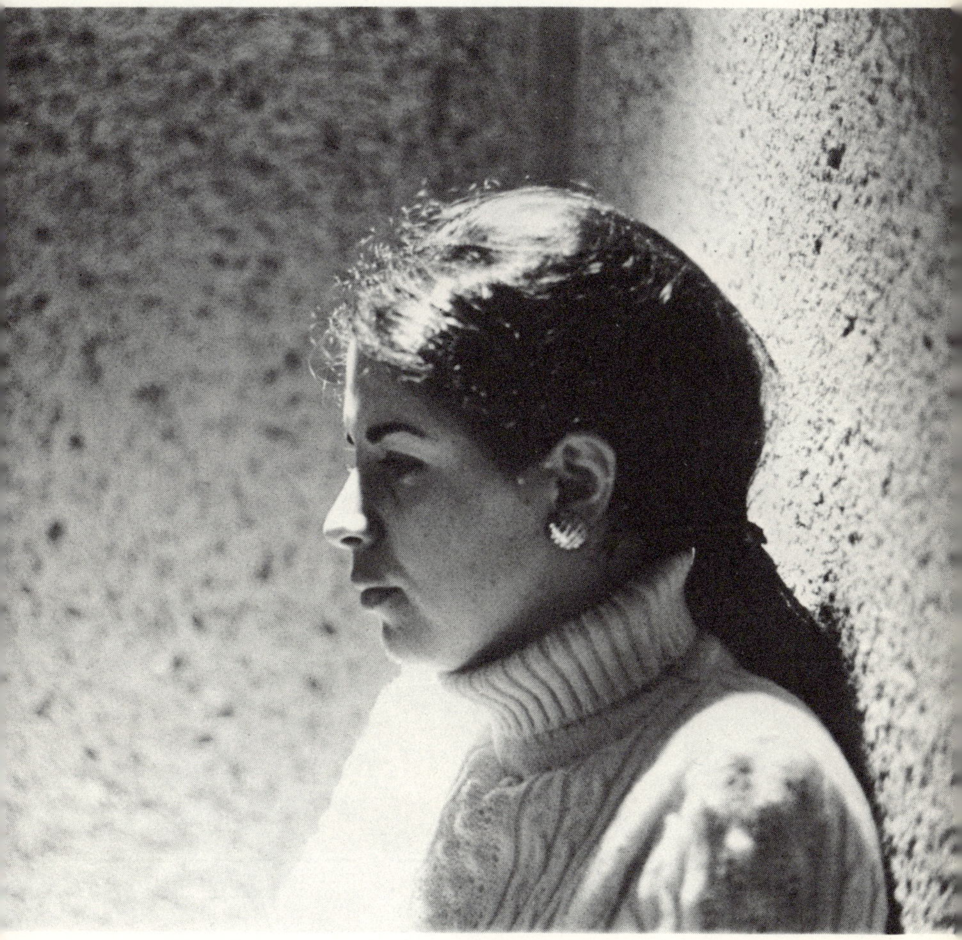

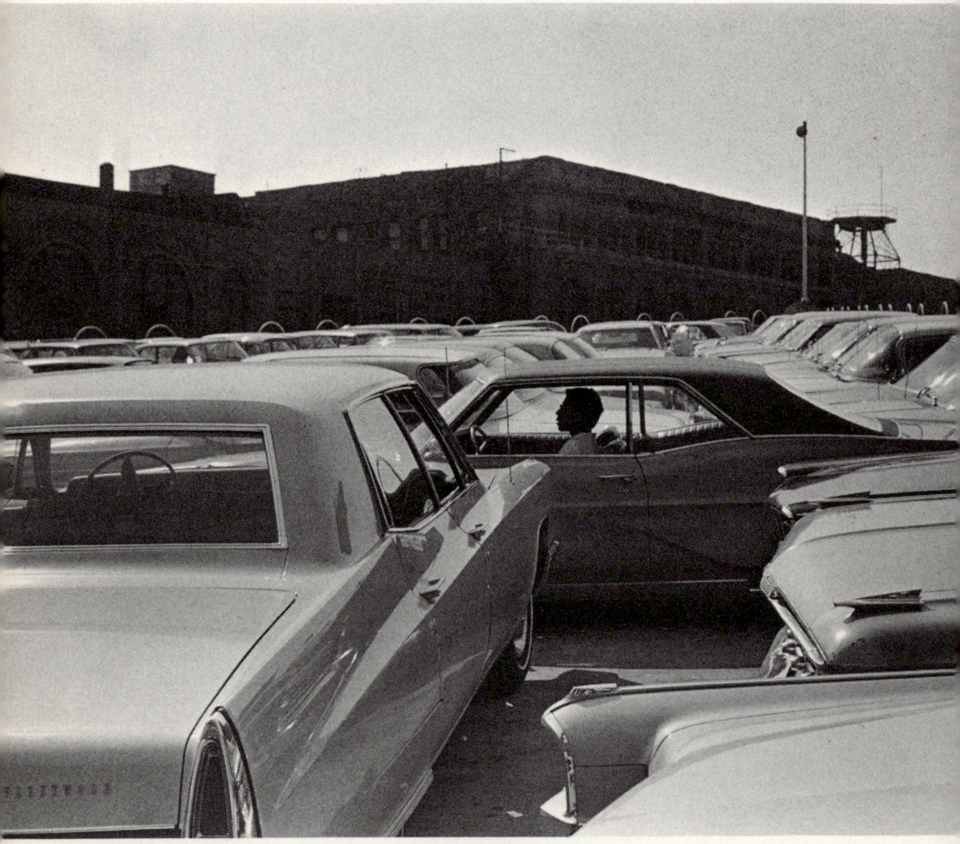

The rationalist tradition,
as the student rebels see it,
has produced a race
of deformed human beings,
or, rather, a race of thinking machines;
heads (the old-fashioned kind)
without bodies or feelings.
The new generation
does not wish men to become mindless;
they wish them to become
something more than minds.

        Martin Duberman

In the "today," in every "today,"
various generations coexist
and the relations which are
established between them,
according to the different
condition of their ages,
represent the dynamic system
of attractions and repulsions,
of agreement and controversy
which at any given moment
makes up the reality of historic life.

      José Ortega y Gasset

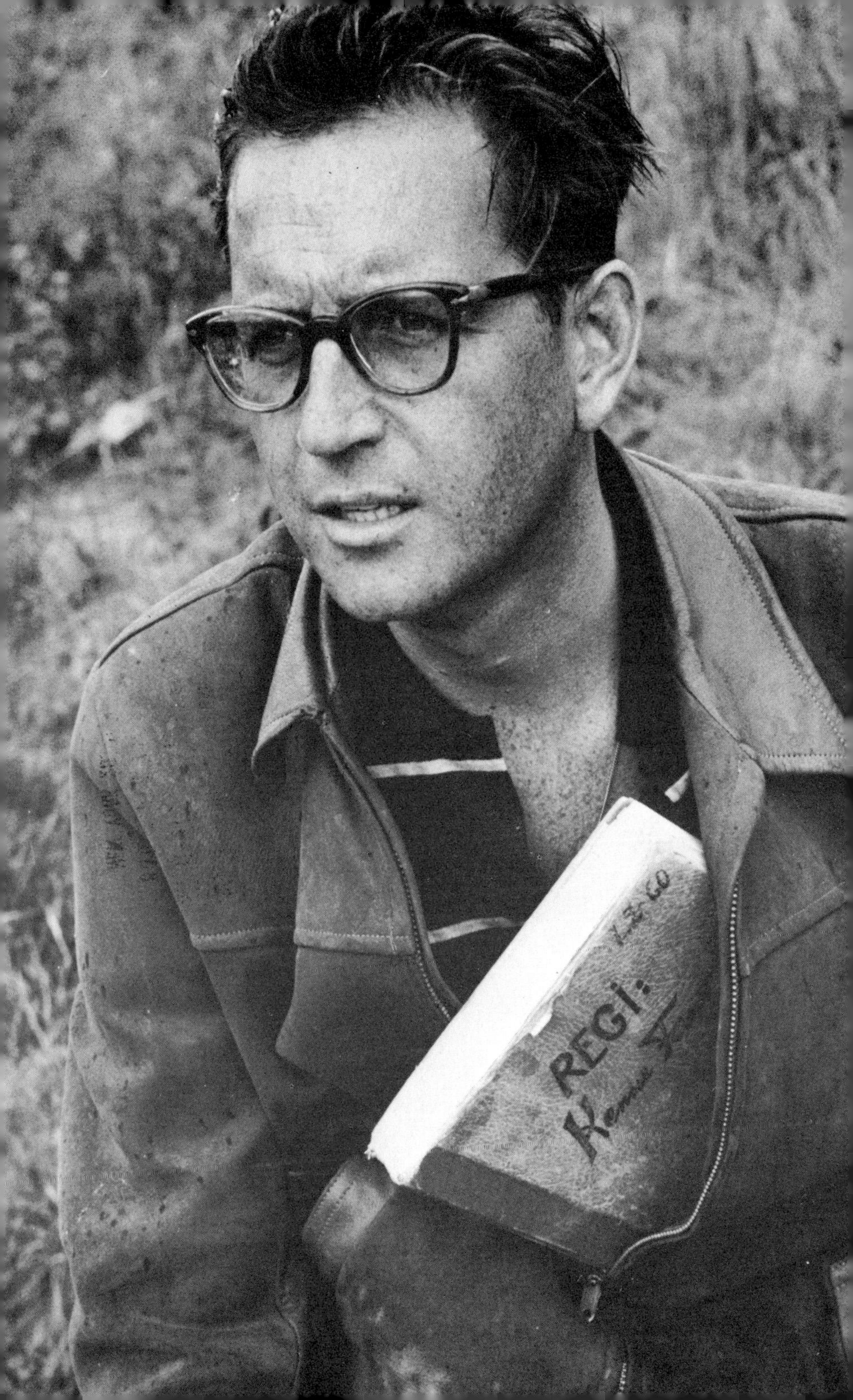
REGI:

7
A NEW HISTORY OF MAN

Teaching and Learning

That adults influence children
is a simple fact of social learning.
A great deal of what we call *personality*
is learned by imitating adults,
as is the case with language;
by absorbing adult interpretations,
as is the case with attitudes
toward policemen and Jews;
by adopting the approved behavior
and eliminating the disapproved ones—
those which are punished in one way or another.
While the source of social learning
is not generally limited to adults,
for young children
adults (parents, teachers) are
the dominant models of
and the chief initiators of
their social learning.

        Hilda Taba

Unfortunately, a degree of prejudice
can be taught easily to all
except those who are
thoroughly trustful and loving.

Benjamin Spock

This is the first generation
of society, anywhere,
so far as I know,
ever to be dedicated
to wiping out all forms
of racial prejudice

  Morris B. Abram

Victory without contending—
how can this be achieved? . . .
It comes the moment the stage is reached
when the enemy no longer sees me
nor I the enemy,
when heaven and earth are yet undivided
and light and shade are one . . .
One must break through
to the world where all things
are essentially of one body.

    Emile Durckheim

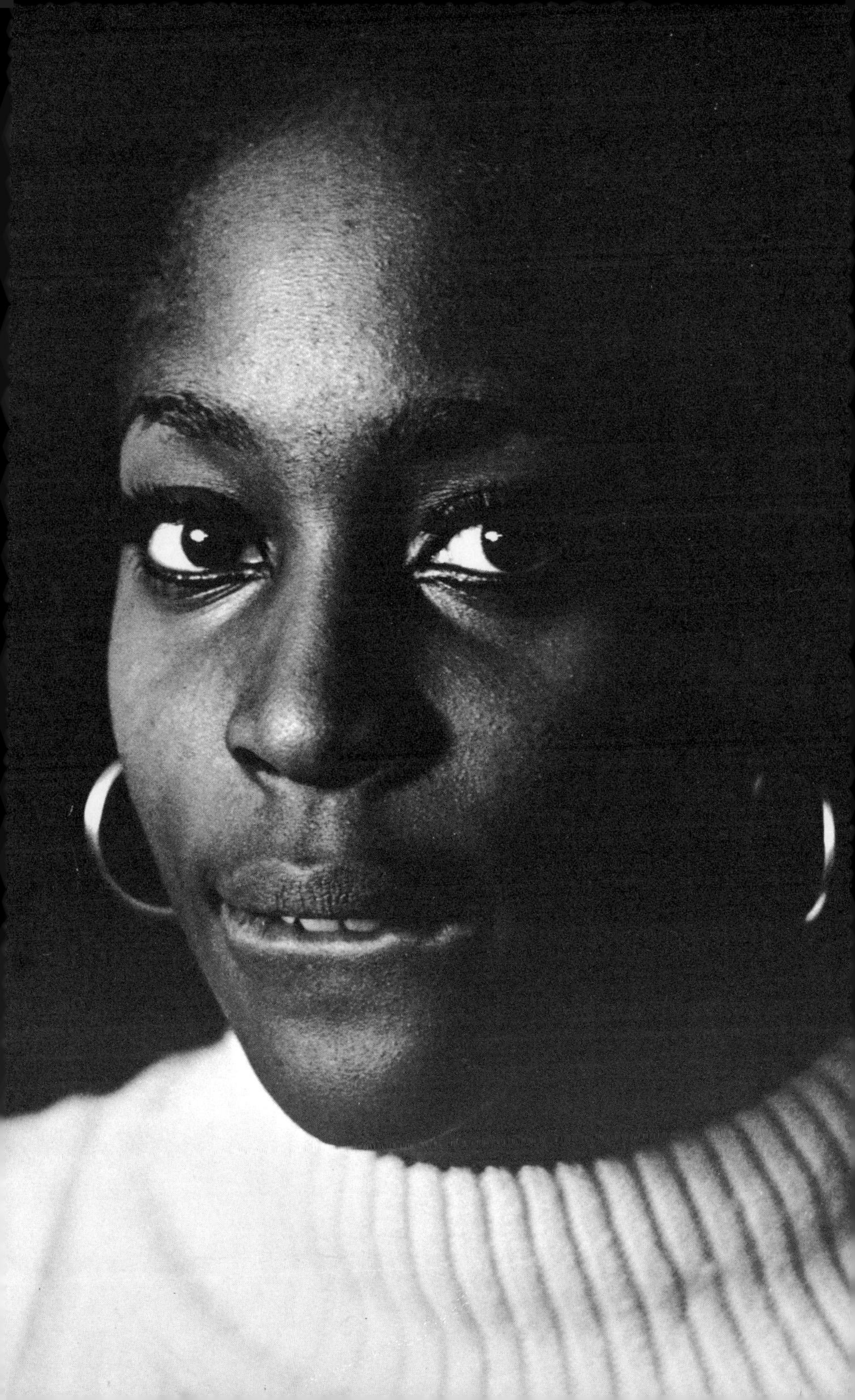

When children are taught tolerance
they do not merely accept it grudgingly.
They respond to it and practice it
with enthusiasm
because it appeals to their
straightforward sense of right.
I know because I've seen it happen,
in families and in good schools.

                Benjamin Spock

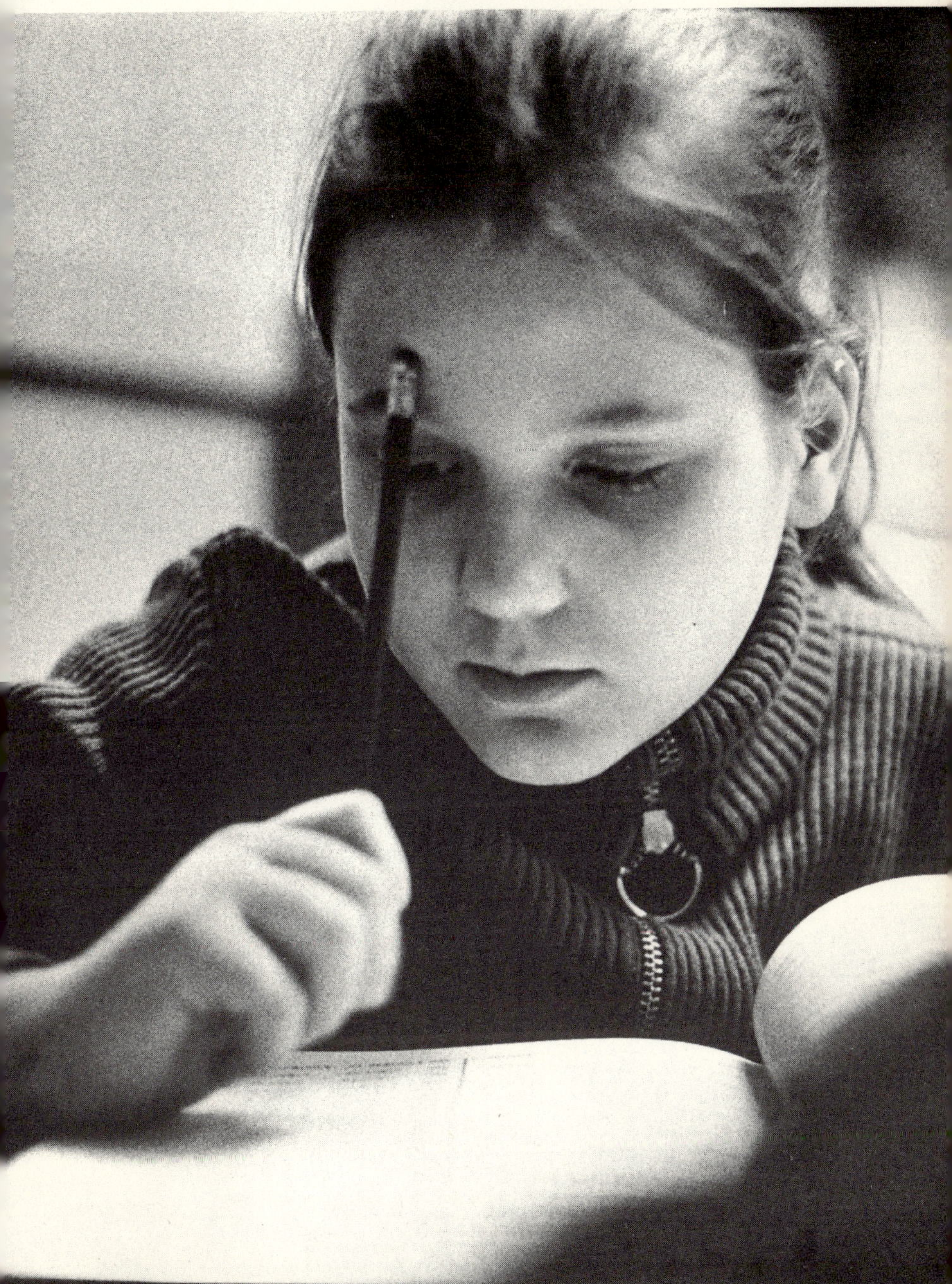

Civilization
is a slow process
of adopting the ideas
of minorities.

Anonymous

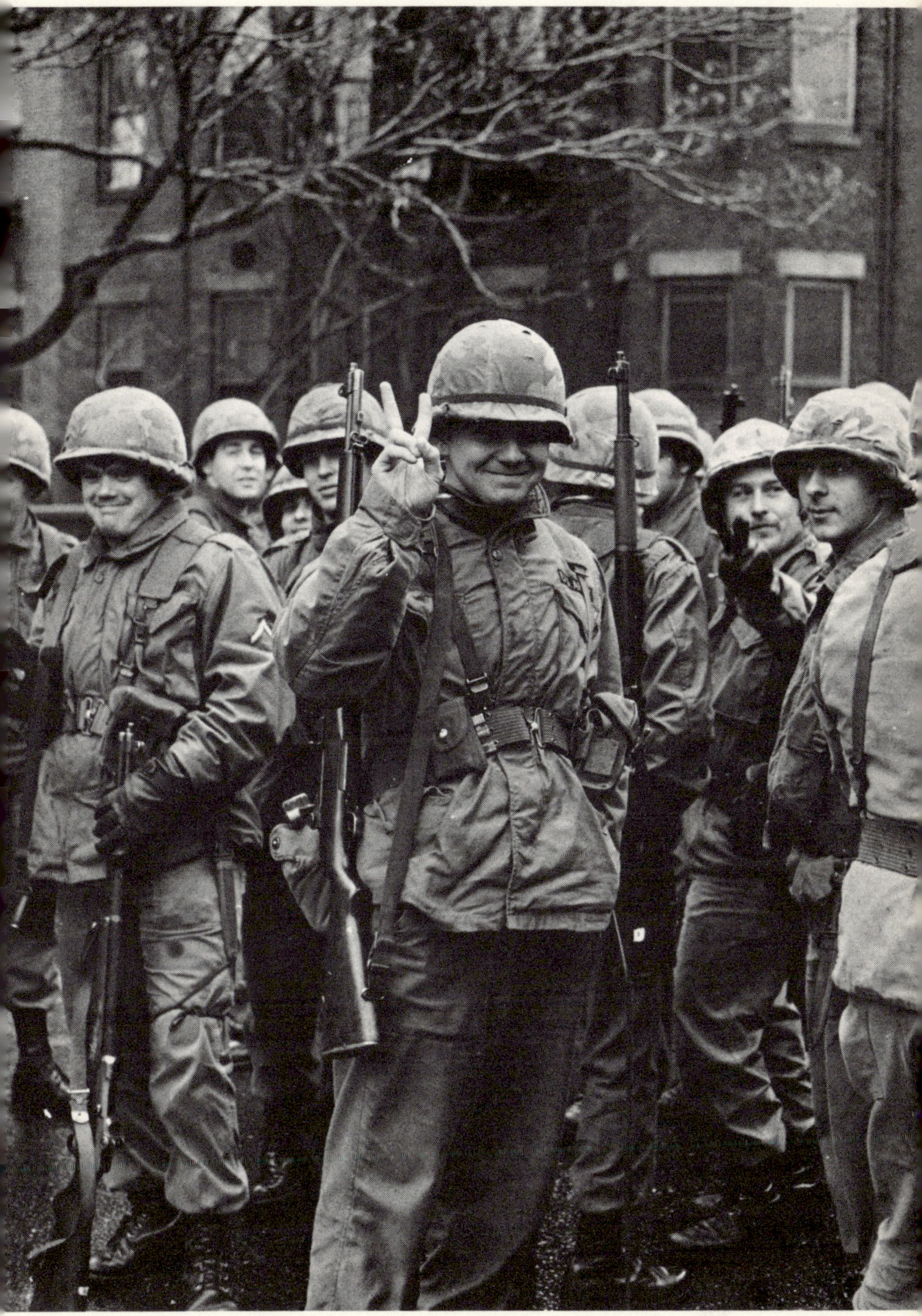

Love with Power

To be courageous requires
no exceptional qualifications,
no magic formula,
no special combination of time,
place, and circumstance.
It is an opportunity
that sooner or later
is presented to us all.

      John F. Kennedy

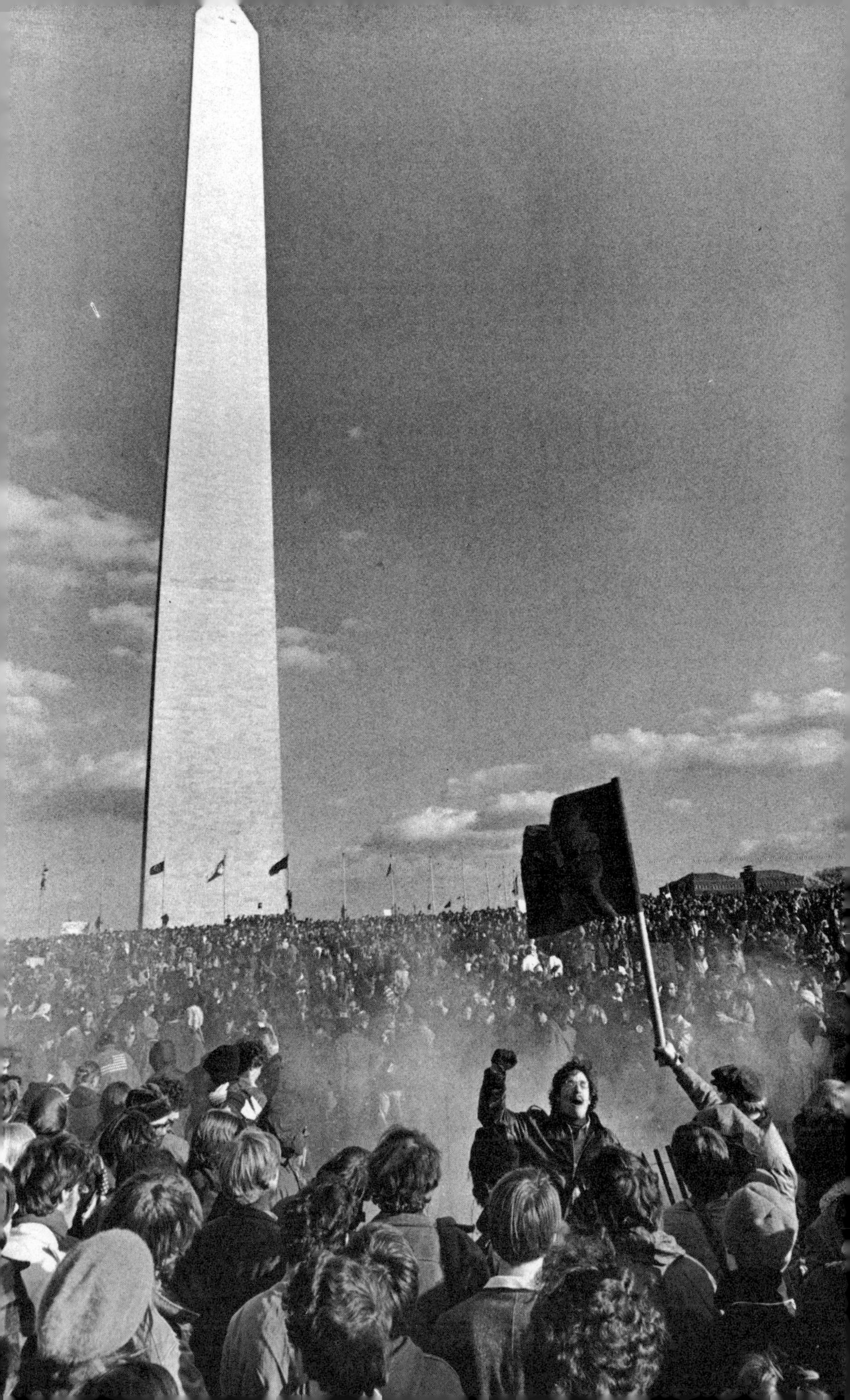

Love without power is not enough,
because love without power
soon ceases to be love.
Without the strength
to resist encroachments,
openness to the other
comes down simply to "giving in."
The person, then, is called to do battle;
there is no advance without it.
If he is also called to know peace,
it is because peace is not a state
but a process,
not just a matter of avoiding conflicts
but of keeping our conflicts constructive.

                Robert O. Johann

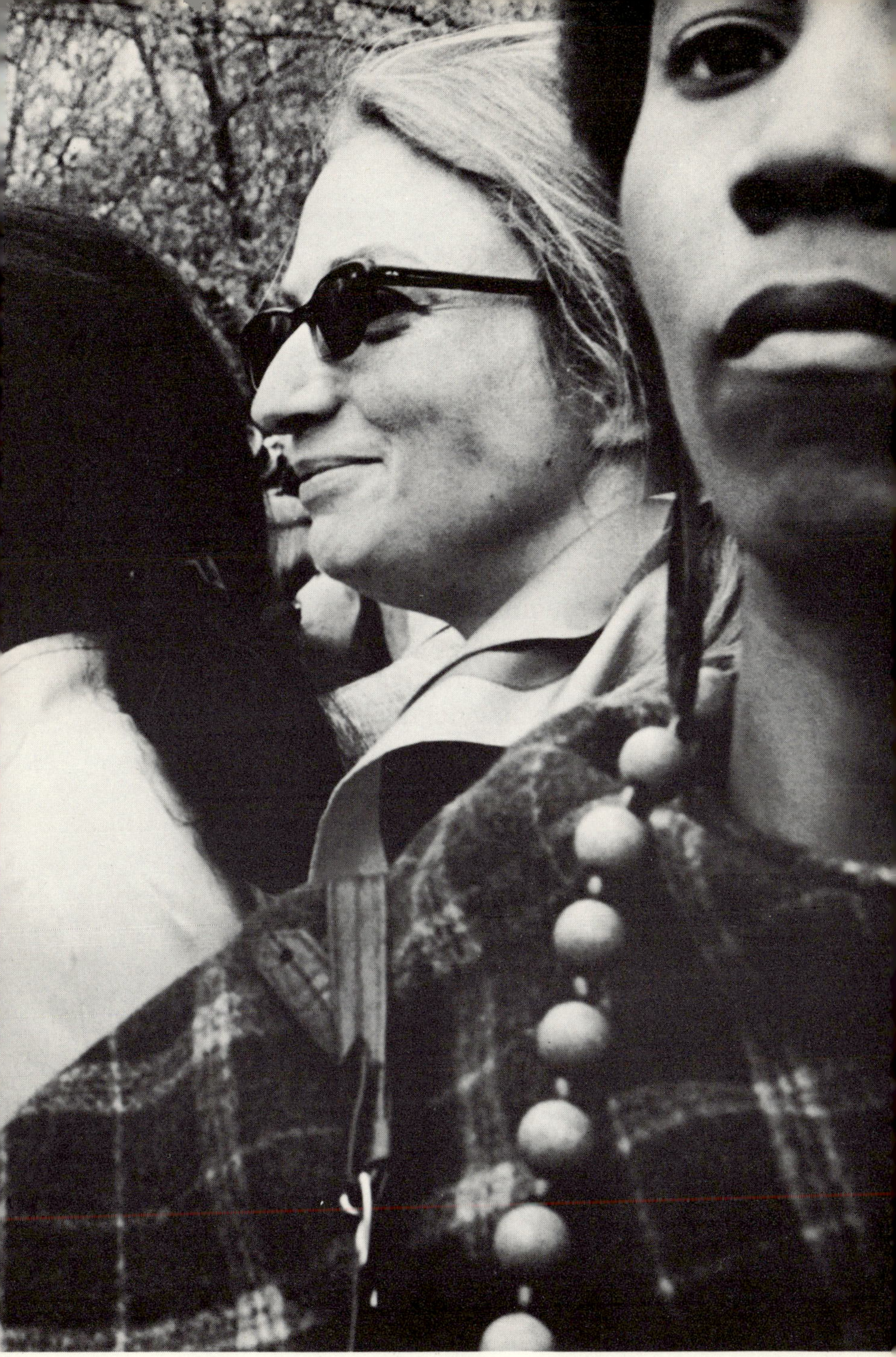

Relentless emphasis on what is wrong,
what is worsening, what is threatening
can lead a people to underestimate
its capacity to control events.
Politics comes increasingly to resemble
what Lenin called an "infantile disorder."
Society regresses to a state
of complaining helplessness
and threatening hysterics.
This sense of society is
not so much unattractive as untrue.
To an astonishing degree
Americans do achieve
the things we set our minds on.

        Daniel P. Moynihan

A great deal
can be done
through the system
by prodding it.

        John Banzhaf

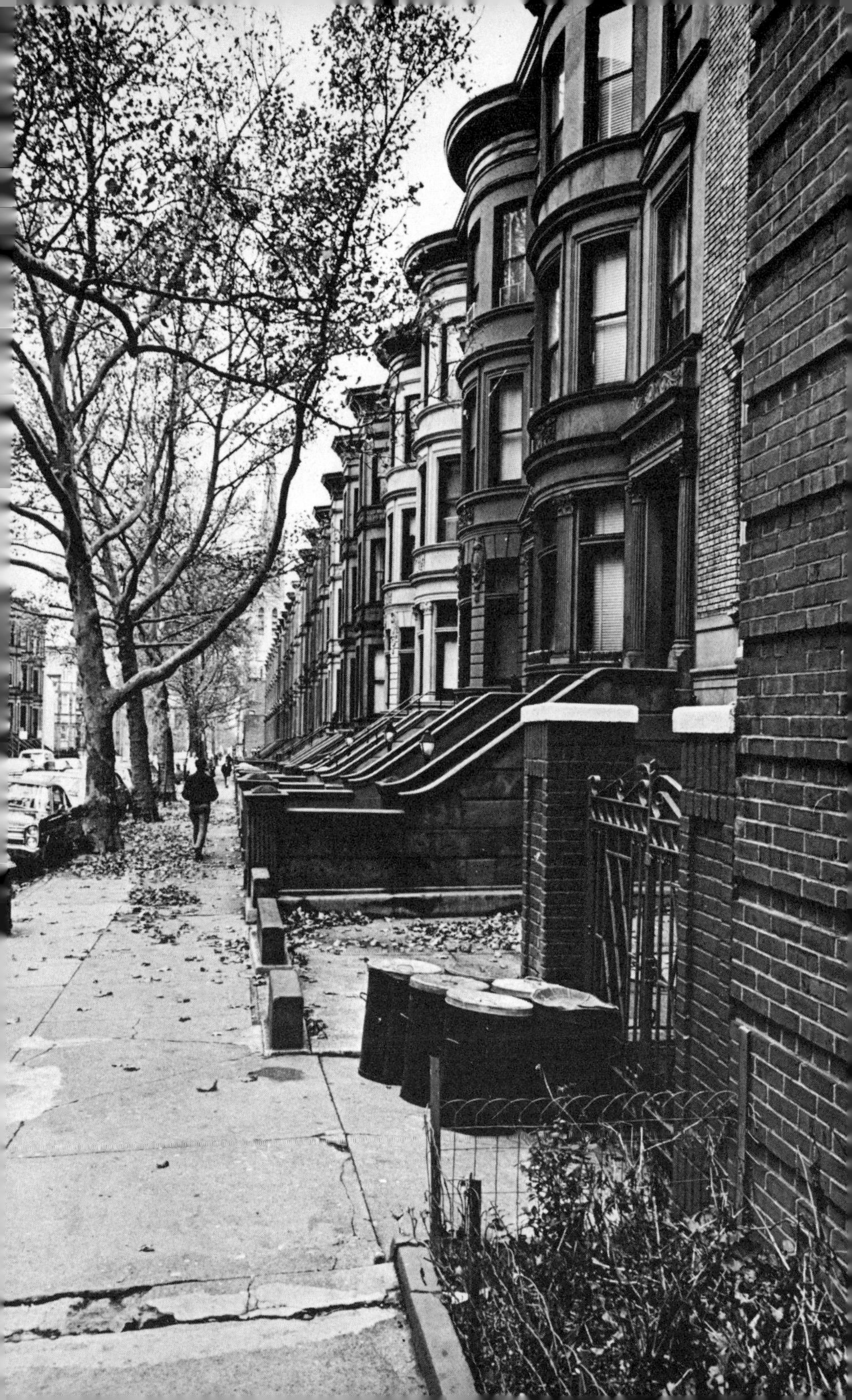

IN THIS TEMPLE
AS IN THE HEARTS OF THE PEOPLE
FOR WHOM HE SAVED THE UNION
THE MEMORY OF ABRAHAM LINCOLN
IS ENSHRINED FOREVER

People must have a hand
in saving themselves;
they cannot and will not
be saved from the outside.

       Gordon W. Allport

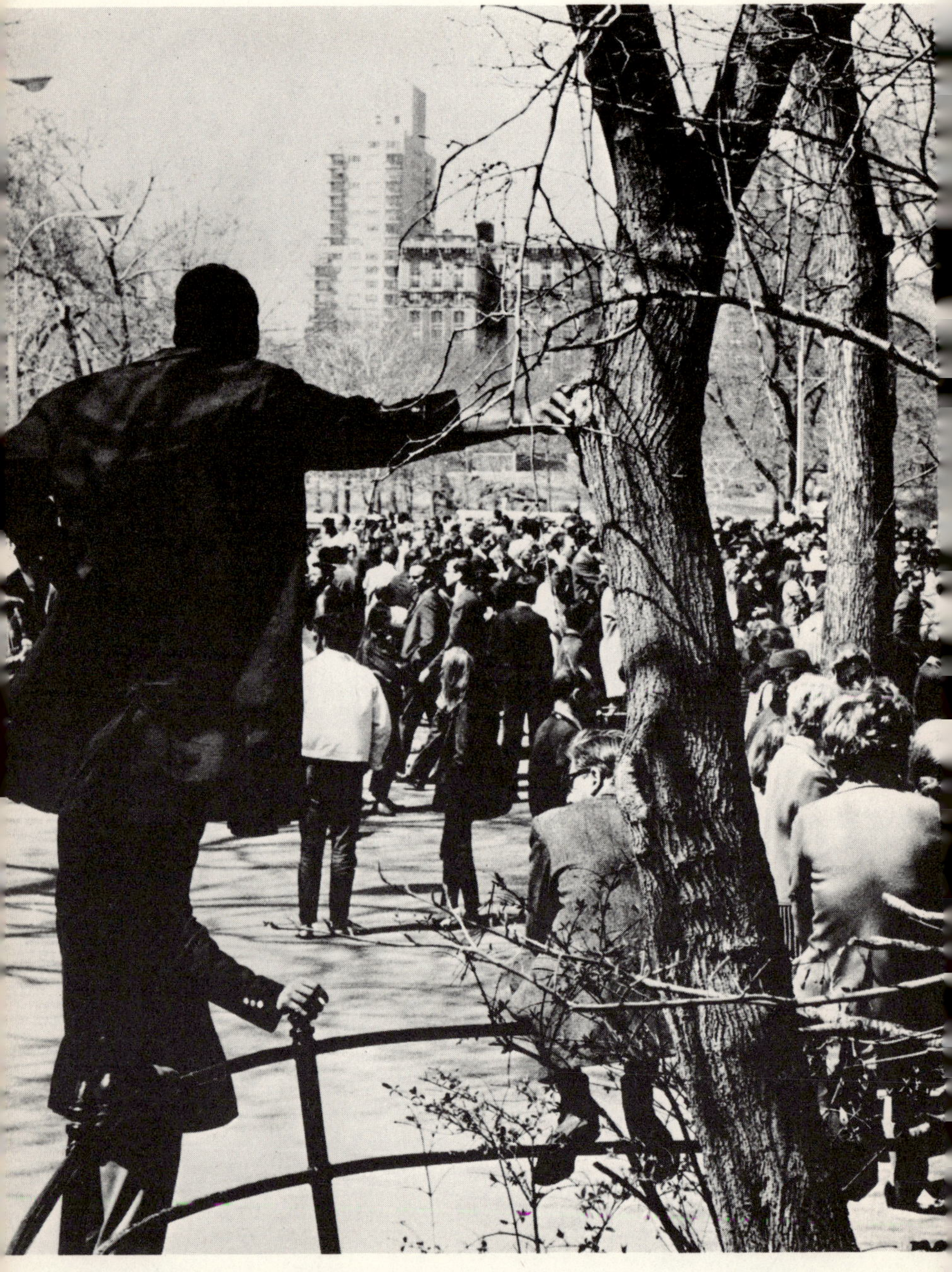

The All Together

Humanity is a symphony
of great collective souls;
and he who understands and loves it
only by destroying a part of those elements,
proves himself a barbarian
and shows his idea of harmony
to be no better than the idea of order
another held in Warsaw ...
Neither family, friend, nor fatherland,
nor aught that we love
has power over the spirit.
The spirit is the light.
It is our duty to lift it
above tempests,
and thrust aside the clouds
which threaten to obscure it;
to build higher and stronger,
dominating the injustice
and hatred of nations,
the walls of that city
wherein the souls of the whole world
may assemble.

    Romain Rolland

I wanted to go to Laos...
As I saw it, the team would consist
only of myself and a few
of the young Americans
who had been with me in North Vietnam.
We would be plain Americans
working among the plain people
of the country,
wherever we were needed.
It would be a simple example
of cooperation
on a people-to-people basis...
The Ambassador shook my hand warmly
and told me that he had confidence in me.
"Many times before," he said,
"white men have come to help us.
But always before
they had other motives:
colonization, trade,
even our religious conversion.
But I really believe that your motive
is a purely human one.
That will make your mission
unique in my country."
Then, he added
with a twinkle in his eye,
"And also, for some of my people,
a little hard to believe."

     Thomas A. Dooley

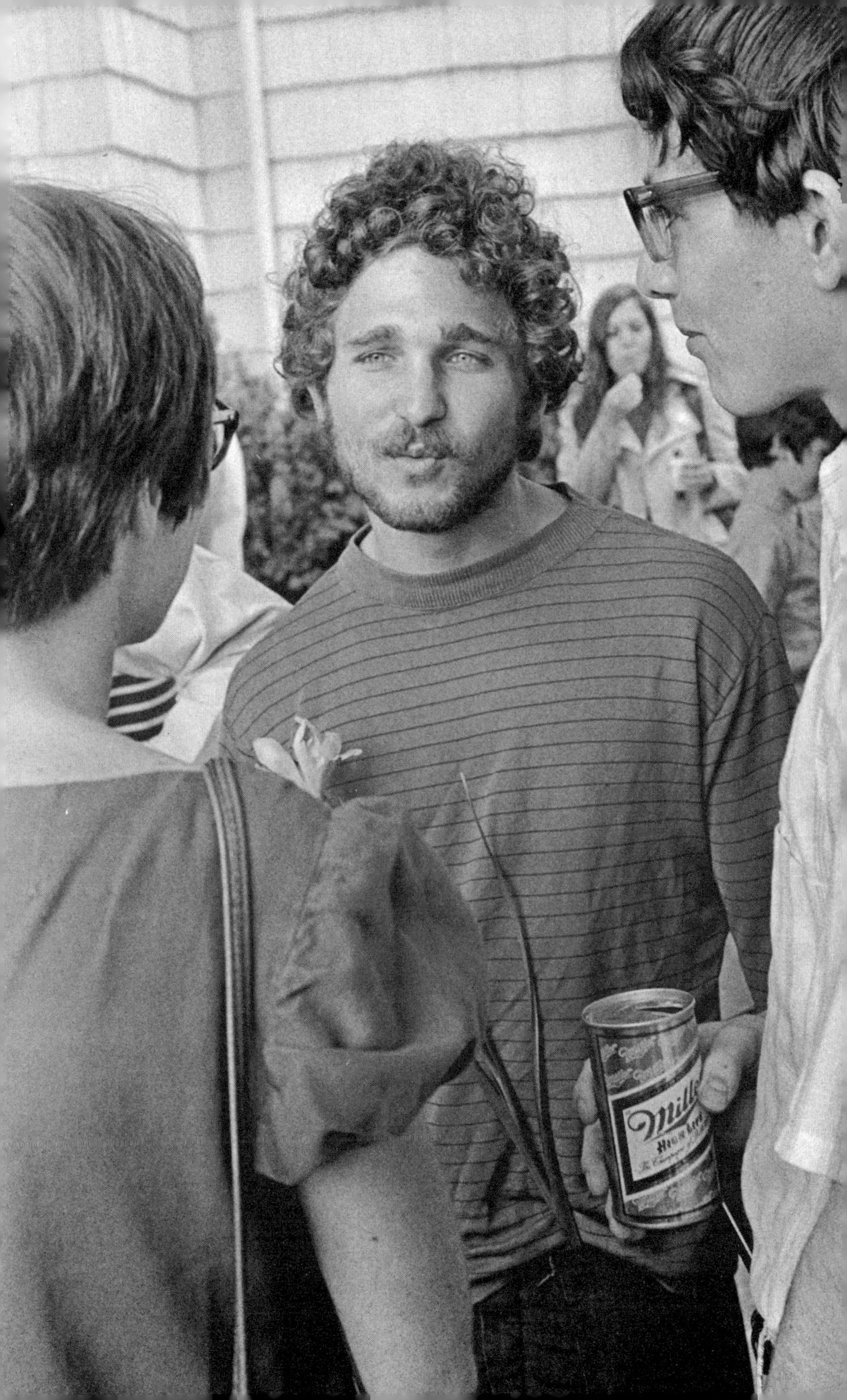

We regard *men* as infinitely precious
and possessed of unfulfilled capacities
for reason, freedom, and love...
We oppose the depersonalization
that reduces human beings
to the status of things.
If anything, the brutalities
of the twentieth century
teach that means and ends
are intimately related,
that vague appeals to "posterity"
cannot justify the mutilations of the present...

Loneliness, estrangement, isolation,
describe the vast distance
between man and man today.
These dominant tendencies
cannot be overcome
by better personnel management,
nor by improved gadgets,
but only when a love of man
overcomes the idolatrous
worship of things by man.

        SDS statement
        Port Huron, 1962

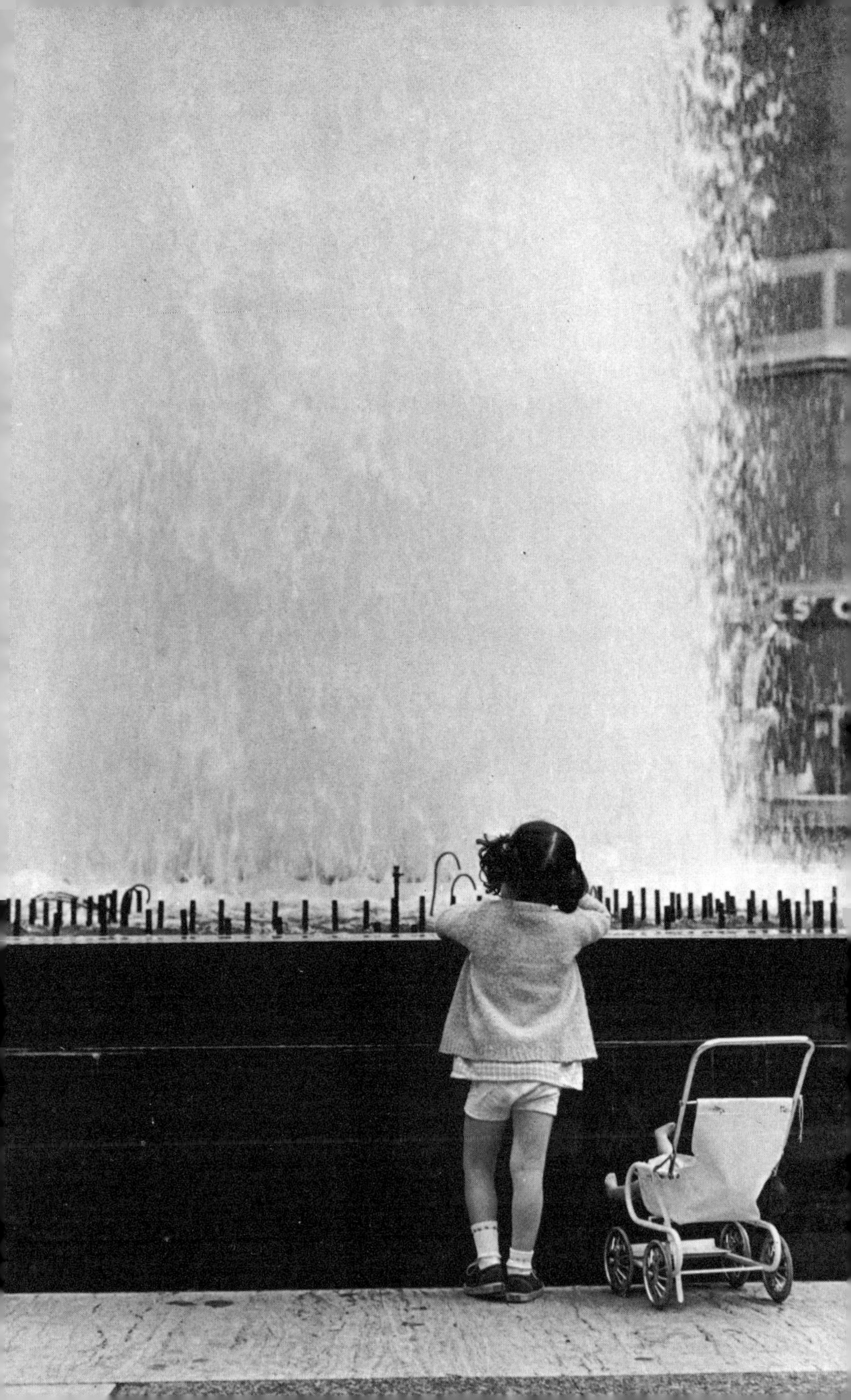

The outcome of the world,
the gates of the future,
the entry into the superhuman—
these are not thrown open
to a few of the privileged
nor to one chosen people
to the exclusion of all others.
They will open to an advance
of *all together*,
in a direction in which *all together*
can join and find completion
in a spiritual renovation of the earth,
a renovation whose physical degree of reality
we must now consider
and whose outline we must make clearer.

        Pierre Teilhard de Chardin

Civilization cannot exist
without new frontiers;
it needs them
both physically
and spiritually ...
The spiritual need ...
in the long run
is more important.

   Arthur C. Clarke

It is a question of the Third World
starting a new history of Man,
a history which will have regard
to the sometimes prodigious theses
which Europe has put forward,
but which will also not forget Europe's crimes,
of which the most horrible
was committed in the heart of man,
and consisted of the pathological
tearing apart of his functions
and the crumbling away of his unity.

        Frantz Fanon

We may speak of a New History
as a period of radical re-creation
of the forms of human culture—
biological, institutional, technological,
experiential, aesthetic, and interpretive.
New cultural forms are not
produced by spontaneous generation;
they are extensions and transformations
of what already exists.
That which is most genuinely revolutionary
makes psychological use of the past
for its plunge into the future.

        Robert Jay Lifton

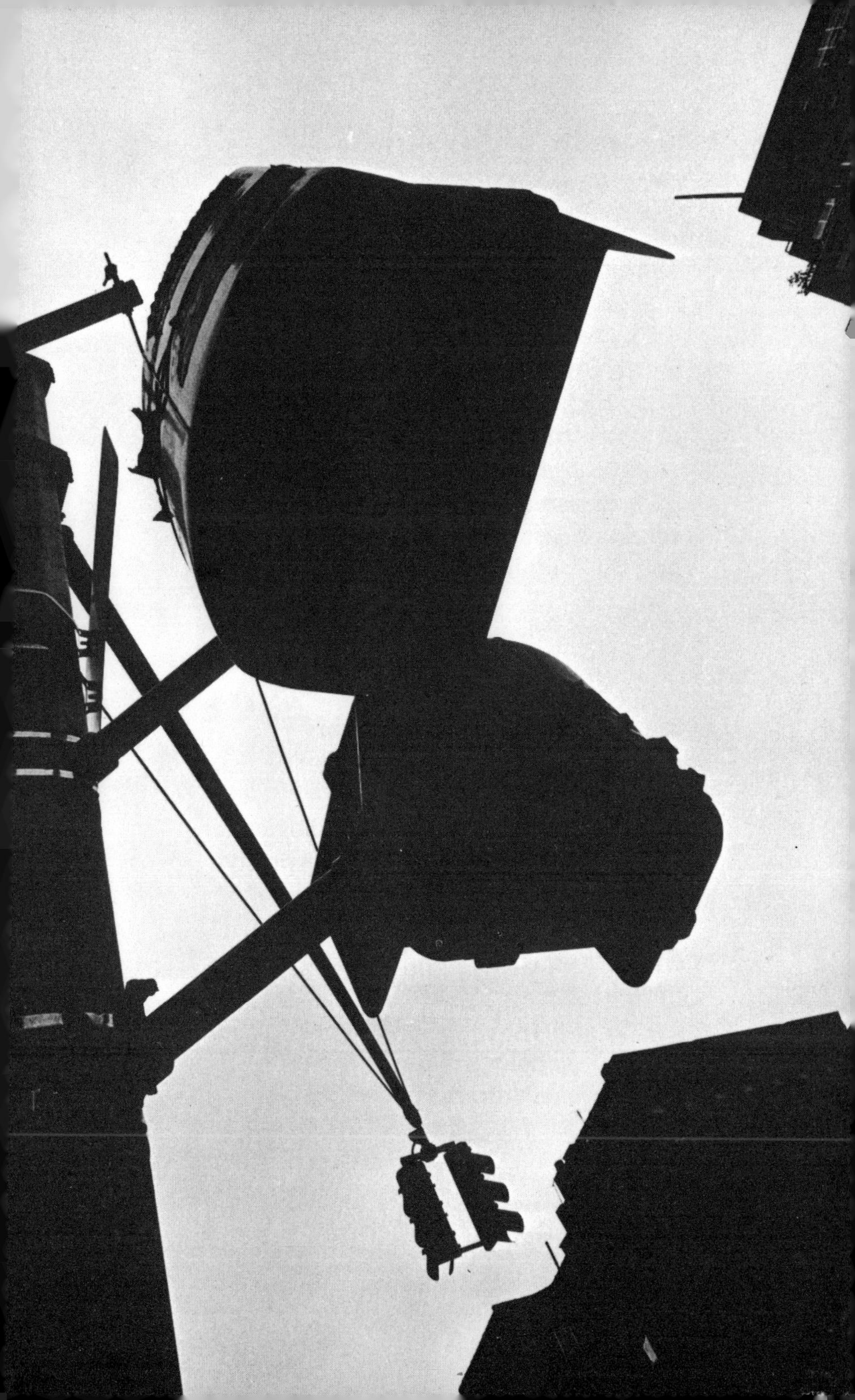